BLAME BLOOM

DIARY OF A DIVORCE LAWYER

LAWRENCE H. BLOOM

BLAME BLOOM

Published by Spines
ISBN: 979-8-89383-751-3

CONTENTS

*To Jo, my co-adventurer, and to Katie and Jake, my daughter and son,
who have each, in their own way, shown me the glory of living.*

*"So, what's the glory in living? Doesn't anybody
ever stay together anymore? And if love never lasts
forever. Tell me, what's forever for?"*

Michael Martin Murphey

This is an ironic quote for a book about divorce, but there you go.

INTRODUCTION

I have been a divorce attorney for the past 40+ years. Throughout that time, I have seen and heard it all.

With apologies to Sy Sperling: I am not only the president of the Divorce Club, but I am also a client.

My approach to practicing matrimonial law has been molded from the framework of a 25-year marriage that was less than satisfactory and ultimately led to my own divorce.

Getting clients, which is always the hardest part of running one's own business, has led me to novel means of client acquisition.

I spent two years hosting an internet radio show every Friday afternoon entitled *"The Divorce Hour,"* addressing all of the myriad issues that interested me as a person undergoing the divorce process (not unlike undergoing surgery) as opposed to strictly legal issues interesting only to an attorney. Quite frankly, the shows that addressed "the law" were the least interesting to me, while the shows focusing on reclaiming one's life were not only fascinating but were the ones garnering the most attention.

I wrote an article published in the *Psychology Today* online blog about *"How My Divorce Made Me a Better Divorce Attorney."*

I even sent out holiday music CDs featuring divorce and breakup songs to friends, family, clients, and prospective clients, as well as to referring attorneys. The "first cut" on each CD was me speaking about my practice and always including the means by which a prospective client could be able to reach me.

I have been interviewed and have conducted interviews.

I even participated as the only attorney in the documentary, *"The Truth About Marriage,"* by director Roger Nygaard, only to wind up on the cutting room floor. I was, however, featured in the accompanying book of the same name by Mr. Nygaard.

I joined various groups: women's rights groups, parent's rights groups, and a father's rights group. At one of these, I met and spoke at length with a movie star who, at the end of the evening, told me to call him if I wanted to represent him. My response was to hand him my business card and tell him to call me if *he* wanted *my* representation. He did. There will be more on him later.

I also joined divorce support groups, often speaking at them and answering questions. Indeed, I was even asked to co-manage a divorce class exploring the various emotional issues of getting on with one's life following separation and divorce.

Needless to say, with more than 40 years in a solo practice as a divorce attorney in New York and New Jersey, I have an interesting perspective on marriage and divorce.

Throughout my career, when telling "war stories" of my cases at cocktail parties, I have often heard, *"You should write a book!"*

As I am now concluding the final phase of my litigation career with retirement in front of me and the proverbial next chapter, I thought now was the appropriate time to write that book.

As is commonplace disclaimer on television shows, *the stories you are about to hear are true; only the names have been changed to protect the innocent,* which in this case is me. There is little if any, embellishment to what you will be reading. It's almost all true! (Part of the game for readers who know me is that they are encouraged to guess what limited parts are fiction.)

I am, of course, bound to keep confidential the matters revealed to me by my clients; and in no instance am I attaching any name to any set of "facts" presented. Indeed, as this is a work of fiction, I admit to taking poetic license – sometimes combining cases, sometimes attributing other lawyer's stories to this, "my story," sometimes altering the "facts," and sometimes making things up entirely.

Writing this book, particularly when relating my personal stories relative to my marriage and divorce, is a cathartic process. It is a form of self-therapy. However, part of the intention of this book is to leave a legacy for my children and granddaughter (as well as for any other grandchildren born after this book's completion). My goal is not to influence them negatively about their mother/grandmother or anyone else.

Throughout my four decades in divorce law, I have often described my profession as *the perfect job for a person in a bad marriage.* Although an apt description, it was always delivered tongue-in-cheek. While not a saint by any means, my wife was not the cause of my divorce. If anything, I was more at fault than she. We grew in different directions and at different rates. Blame Bloom; blame me.

At the outset, I must also tell you that I am not flippant about divorce. It is a terrible thing. I have been through it on a personal level and have had many members of my family and friends go through the process of divorce.

As you read, please understand that I do not take what I do lightly.

I really believe that what I do helps people.

Certainly, other areas of the law would have proven to be more remuneratively rewarding.

I have always been able to let my sense of humor be my flashlight out of the darkness.

As you will read, my career has had ups and downs, but it has never been dull.

CHAPTER 1
DIVORCE LAW

Why divorce law?

Yes, there is something called the Matrimonial Bar; and most of my colleagues call themselves family lawyers or matrimonial attorneys.

The truth is that those other names are euphemisms.

Divorce is a dirty business.

Clients seeking a divorce or representation in a non-marital family issue are people experiencing the worst the world can offer – the most trusted of relationships gone bad.

Only the death of a child – and having seen my parents lose my only sibling 20 years ago, that, too, the result of a disgustingly bad divorce – is more traumatic than the death of a marriage.

So, I have always defined my professional self by what I really do.

I fight the battles that need to be fought. I get down in the gutter when necessary. I do what I need to do to get the best results for my client. One of my mottos has always been: *I don't practice law to make friends; I do it to represent my clients.*

Pragmatically, I want each case to settle. Every case not

involving the custody of children should be settled. Everything else is just money. Money can be compromised, particularly when the two sides are each paying someone to resolve the money issues. There comes a time when the costs of litigation outweigh even a best-case financial victory. No case should involve $100,000 in legal fees. Yet I have been involved in family dissolution matters involving legal fees (to the other side's lawyers) in the millions. In fact, one law firm declared me its Man of the Year for the millions of dollars in fees they generated by responding to my actions on behalf of my clients.

Another media-hungry divorce lawyer was able to purchase his Rolls Royce based upon fees generated because my client, the wife of his doctor-client, was so vengeful after the husband left her for his nurse, conducted her life in such a way that screamed, *"YOU LEFT ME FOR THAT TRAMP! YOU ARE NEVER GOING TO SEE THE KIDS AGAIN!"* (*"That Tramp!"* is not an uncommon reference by a wife in a divorce action.) The husband was never going to accept that, resulting in hundreds of thousands of dollars in legal fees.

Even cases involving children should usually be settled. Everyone knows the story of King Solomon and his suggestion that the baby be cut in half.

The truth is that when you have children, you may become legally divorced; but that final decree never ends the family. There will be milestone events for your children: birthdays, graduations, marriages, and then grandchildren; and there are other health and career issues for your children that require both divorced parents to interact. You will always be a family. Your paths will always cross.

It takes two to make a baby; and it should take two to raise that child. Except in rare instances, joint custody with the concomitant joint decision-making on all major issues impacting that child should be the norm (although the opposite has always been true in the Courts). The issue of parenting time is what most custody disputes center on, and that is a matter rife for compromise.

A trial of a divorce case – and particularly where custody and visitation are in issue – only metastasizes the cancer of the decaying relationship with your spouse or co-parent, thereby making future interactions all the more troublesome for you, for your children, and for your (eventual) grandchildren.

Of course, people going through a divorce are at the worst points of their lives. Reason and future relations with your spouse are not always at the forefront. Indeed, a future relationship with the soon-to-be ex is not even the smallest of considerations. The truth is that no one gets married to get divorced, and no one gets a divorce with the thought of maintaining a future relationship with their soon-to-be ex.

I have been compelled to try highly contested cases and been involved in the almost-always follow-up appellate practice. These cases have resulted in the six- and seven-figure legal fees. These cases have also inevitably resulted in a future for the litigants just as bad as the marriage.

Life is a series of negotiations. Divorce, like life itself, requires negotiation from strength as opposed to weakness. Hit 'em hard and hit 'em fast, so that the other party and the other lawyer will know at the very beginning that the negotiations should begin in earnest as soon as possible. Often, the best defense truly is the best offense.

Much as someone seeking medical treatment for a life-threatening disease wants a "guarantee" for a cure, so too do clients – and in particular matrimonial clients – seek guarantees on the results of litigation. No lawyer should ever guarantee short of those involving death and taxes, but that never stops the demand for a guarantee. My next come-back is: "You want a guarantee? There are only three guarantees I can make.

(1) You can find a lawyer who charges more than me.

(2) You can find a lawyer who charges less than me.

(3) If you want, I can handle your case in such a way that I can guarantee you will never reconcile."

That last guarantee sets me apart from every other attorney.

Throughout my 40+ year career as a high-conflict divorce lawyer, I have always let the Judge know that Bloom is ready to litigate, to try the case if necessary, but that settlement is always the best alternative. This approach has gained me the respect of the Matrimonial Bench.

Indeed, on one occasion, I presented what is known as an *ex parte* application to a trial judge whom I had known for many years. I presented a motion where I asked for emergency relief; on requests of this nature, the other side is advised within 24 hours of the appearance and can show up or not (although I consider it legal malpractice to allow *any* aspect of my client's case to be heard without my input). On this particular occasion, I was alone with the Judge and her staff. After we addressed the case that presented the reason for my appearance, the Judge asked where we were on my "other" case and whether a settlement was a possibility – which we both knew was a hotly contested matter that had already been the subject of two interim appeals and which was scheduled for trial a few weeks later. I told the judge, *"Your Honor, last week was my birthday. What do you think I wished for when I blew out the candles?"*

The biggest compliments I ever received were when Judges before whom I had had matters chose me to become their divorce lawyer, with those Judges who referred their family and friends to me being a category not too far behind.

But 40 years is a long time; Judges come and go. I did not realize that until Judges with whom I had first been acquainted as only lawyers joined the Bench and later ultimately retired while I continued to practice. Nevertheless, the new ones speak with the old ones. They talk with each other about their own war stories, the unusual fact patterns, the lawyers, and sometimes even the clients.

The reputation a lawyer makes lasts a lifetime.

I would like to think that while a judge may not have liked me – and believe me, there have been many that have not – they all had at least a grudging respect for me.

CHAPTER 2
MY JOURNEY

I ASK AGAIN: Why divorce law?

No, this is not a typo.

This is the question: How did I get here? What made me choose an area of the law that is so dirty? What made me choose an area of the law where I truly earned every dollar I ever made?

For that matter, why the law at all?

For that, I go back to the beginning.

Like every good Jewish boy growing up on Long Island in the Baby Boomer Generation, I was brought up to be a professional. *"A doctor, an accountant, or a lawyer will never go hungry,"* my parents always told me. *"A professional will always be able to get a job."*

With an affinity for math and science (at least through elementary and high school, all of which deserted me in college), it seemed preordained that I would be premed in college.

I was. Emphasis on the past tense. More accurately, I *started* college as a premed.

Then two things happened, almost simultaneously.

First semester sophomore year at an Ivy League institution, I took organic chemistry lab. This was the downfall of many premeds. It was certainly my downfall. The class, which was separate from the large (hundreds of students in a large lecture hall) taught by a professor, was a small class often taught by a graduate student called a teaching assistant where students performed experiments relating to the lecture topics. My teaching assistant was a dead ringer for Jane Hathaway from the old *Beverly Hillbillies* television show.

Six weeks into an eight-week experiment (Tuesdays and Thursdays, 8:00 to 10:00 a.m.), we were instructed to *"add two drops of dilute hydrochloric acid."* Guess who forgot to dilute his hydrochloric acid?

The result was a literal explosion, destroying not only my project but that of the person across from me, the people on each side of me, and the people across from them.

"Take off your pants," yelled Jane Hathaway, not Anne Hathaway. In shock and without thinking, I did as I was told and removed my brand-new Levi's only to find the zipper remaining. The acid took the rest of the pants.

The D-minus I ultimately received in that course was a gift of two credits.

But by then, the second thing had happened; and my future career in the sciences was history.

As a premed with a plan to apply to medical schools shortly, I had to build up my resume which meant that during the same semester as the organic chemistry fiasco, I took on a volunteer position at the local hospital.

While working with a 300-pound paralyzed woman, I uttered the one four-letter word that is taboo in a hospital. Through no fault of my own, this woman slipped out of my hands while I was transferring her from bed to a wheelchair. Although I was able to catch her before disaster struck, I did let the word *"Oops"* come out of my lips. Evidently, that is the worst four-letter word in a hospital.

End of job in the hospital. End of my then-existing career goal.

What would I do? What would I become when I grew up?

The math major that I had originally declared had ended even earlier than my premedical aspirations when my first Professor in third-semester calculus (I had completed first-year college math in high school) was Pakistani. It took me a month before I could understand enough of his accent to realize that he was talking about *"a nice function;"* and it took another month to figure out that a *"nice function"* was a function that *"does what you want it to do."* A "function" itself is one that only a math nerd can truly understand. As a former high school Mathlete entering college with sophomore standing in mathematics at a prestigious Ivy League university, I thought I was sufficiently nerdy to grasp these concepts. Apparently, I was not the nerd I considered myself to be – at least not in math.

So, there I was, lost at sea, having no idea what was going on.

I went to my roommate who had not only placed out of first year math, but had placed out of all of his first-year classes. Did I mention that he was only 15 years old (or the fact that his father was the Chairman of the Physics Department)? He was intimidating and neither of us ever formed a bond with the other. He thought my predicament was hilarious. Blame Bloom.

So, math was out. So, quite obviously, was science.

But I am not going to lie, the spring semester of sophomore year was liberating and exhilarating. I got to explore departments in my college and other colleges at my university. I took the classes that interested me.

Ultimately, I became an economics major for several different reasons, not the least of which was that economics had the least number of required classes than any other major. But I was very interested in the field.

I then decided that I would become an antitrust prosecutor.

Little did I know. I would not realize until the end of law school, and after publishing a Law Review article in which antitrust and environmental laws were the subject, that there were only two employers *in the world*. I interviewed with the U.S. Justice Department (they didn't want me) and never heard back from the Federal Trade Commission. [While on Law Review, I first exhibited my desire to work on my own. The editor-in-chief, a third-year law student while I was a mere second-year, told the troops that each of us was to devote at least an hour a day to writing our respective articles. Privately, I told him that that was *"not the way I worked."* I told him that I could write for as many as 10 hours on any given day but that I was not going to be on a schedule and would not write when I did not feel I could be productive. My way proved correct as I was the first of my year to publish. I doubt that anyone other than myself and my editor made it through the entire article. My parents, well-educated with degrees from Wharton and the University of Wisconsin, each tried to read it but never made it past the title.]

But with antitrust prosecution as my declared future, I had a career goal.

That pointed me toward law school. Not Harvard. I used to tell my fellow law students, *"If I could spell, I'd be at Harvard."* I think the organic chemistry lab grade and its impact on my grade point average more likely limited the law schools that would even consider me.

As a college graduate in 1976, with a liberal arts economics degree, I realized that I was woefully unprepared to enter the real world.

It was either law school or business school. A Master's in Business Administration (MBA) would offer a lucrative career in Corporate America; a score on my business boards in the top 2% of the nation (far better than the score on my law boards) offered me entry into the top business schools. Unfortunately, each application had a single question I could not answer: Why do you want to go to business school? Other than *"to make a lot of money,"* I never had an answer. Those applications were never completed let alone submitted.

At least with law schools, I had an answer to the "why" question. My answer had nothing to do with what I would eventually become when I entered the professional world, but it was an answer.

I then became a law graduate, passed the Bar Exam, and looked for a job.

Having no idea of what area of the law was to be my future, I looked for jobs in the small town where I went to law school only to be offered jobs paying less than I could make as a waiter (far less than $200 per week).

At the time, one of my neighbors was a reporter for the local newspaper. She wrote a feature on my plight, with my face appearing at the top of the front page on the second section of the paper under the heading, *"Larry Bloom, the Lawyer, is Having Trouble Finding a Job."* This was a source of amusement for my friends for many years. Indeed, a copy of it was presented to me at the roast of me that served as a bachelor party.

Unable to secure meaningful employment in the small city where I had attended law school, I went home to Mom and Dad, where at least I would not have to pay rent and where food was on the table.

I looked for jobs as an attorney in New York City and on Long Island, ultimately finding a job in Forest Hills in Queens with a general practicing attorney who handled all kinds of legal matters. My boss was well into his 80s (he would probably be around 125 years old were he alive today); and I essentially served as his legs.

I did everything that required being out of the office, which meant all litigation, including criminal matters, personal injury, and divorce, and I did real estate closings and interviewed clients in jail.

Oh God, did I hate going to work!

Personal injury was the science I had given up early in college. That was a nonstarter.

Real estate was boring. So boring in fact that many years later my secretary threatened to quit if I ever took on another real estate matter – and at that time we were doing a refinancing for her mother for free.

Criminal law was not right for me. I thought that if I made a mistake, an innocent man's liberty would be taken away. The nail in that coffin was when I interviewed a client of the firm in the Queens Men's House of Detention late Friday afternoon on Memorial Day weekend, with the only thought in my mind being that there would be a shift change for the guards and that I would be locked up until the following Tuesday.

Throughout my career, I was fond of saying that "my entire criminal law practice was *pro bono.*" I only took cases of the children of friends and family – the people I could neither say no to nor charge a fee.

I had done some bankruptcy as a law clerk during my law school days; and that didn't do it for me either.

But with divorce, I made a difference. My clients needed me. They spoke with me often. Most of them did so daily. Some, more than daily. In rare instances, only weekly. This was in sharp contrast to my other clients who could go weeks or even months without any communication or concern for their case.

There was really no other alternative in the law for me than a specialty or concentration in divorce and family law.

The next step was a new job.

Here is where I got lucky. My mom, God rest her soul, came to my rescue.

The truth is that an entire book could be devoted to my mother, who, after having two boys, obtained a post-graduation degree in education and special education. She worked throughout my childhood in that field without ever losing her sense of humor, and I can still hear her voice saying, *"If you have nothing nice to say, come sit next to me."*

At the time that my mother came to my professional rescue, Mom was a headhunter. She placed legal secretaries. It is a terrible state of affairs that a headhunter in this country is more financially remunerative than the far more important job of being a special education teacher.

In any event, Mom was cold calling one day, when a lawyer told her, *"I don't need a secretary, but I do need a matrimonial attorney."* Mom's response was classic: *"I've got good news and better news. My son is a new attorney wanting to specialize in matrimonial law; and you don't have to pay me a commission!"*

Full-time divorce law in Manhattan was my future set to begin after giving my two-week notice.

For the first time, I was excited about going to work. I went into a contested matrimonial practice which concentrated in high conflict matters.

CHAPTER 3
THE CONCENTRATION

There are strict ethical rules about a lawyer referring to him/herself as a "specialist." I have never been certified as a matrimonial specialist. However, the fact remains that from the summer of 1980 through my retirement, I did little else but divorce and family law-related matters.

The various Ethics committees prefer the term "concentration;" so that is what I have been, a lawyer who has concentrated his career on divorce law.

Being young in 1980 and a newbie in my field (not yet even admitted to practice in the Courts of New Jersey, which would not come until four years later) turned out not to be a disadvantage. On July 19, 1980, New York's Equitable Distribution Law went into effect. This was literally within days of my taking this new job as a matrimonial attorney.

As I started practice in New York (and only admitted to practice law in New Jersey five years later), I will mostly address the law as it applies in New York. However, although terms may be different between States, the laws are similar – but not exactly the same.

Although a little dry, I must digress into some history of divorce law.

New York has important dates in the history of matrimonial law. Before the 1960s (before even my time), adultery was the only ground for divorce. This resulted in people going to Reno, Nevada, Mexico, and Haiti to get their divorces. You might remember the song, *Haitian Divorce*, by Steely Dan.

Most surprisingly, adultery was and still remains to this day (!) a Class B misdemeanor; it's a crime! Adultery is defined as having sexual relations where one of the parties to the act is married to a non-participant. In other words, even if you are single or divorced, if your sexual partner is married at the time of the act, you are guilty of committing adultery regardless of whether or not you knew of your partner's marital status because adultery is a non-intent crime. You could go to jail for it, although could you imagine the political commercials during election season when an incumbent had wasted tax-payer money prosecuting adultery? This may explain why it has been about 50 years since there has been an adultery prosecution in Manhattan.

But those foreign divorces – and Nevada is a "foreign state" in the eyes of the law – were only good for one thing: getting the divorce itself.

As I have been telling clients throughout my career spanning four decades, the divorce is the easy part. The hard parts of the divorce process were and are the ancillary issues: What is the custody and visitation arrangement with children; how much alimony and child support is to be paid and for what length of time, and how will the property of the parties be distributed?

My practice has always been involved with contested divorces. In fact, one would describe my cases as hotly contested.

Statistically, very few divorce matters went to trial. Nationwide, roughly 2% of all divorces are tried to decision by the court. Far fewer went to the appellate courts.

In marked contrast, throughout my years, I was trying as many as 20% of the cases that came to me. As a young lawyer working for a seasoned matrimonial trial lawyer, that was what we did; we tried cases. When we got decisions that we did not like, we took appeals and often asked the appellate tribunal for interim relief pending resolution of the entire appeal, which could take months or even years. Indeed, at one point, I was in the Appellate Division, Second Department (there are four departments throughout the State of New York with one in Manhattan, one in Brooklyn, and the other two "upstate") that when I walked into the Clerk's Office, I was greeted with *"Hi Larry. What do you have for us today?"* I was that much of a regular in that Court.

As time went on and I was no longer an employee, my percentages for trial and appeal dropped significantly. When I sat on the boss' side of the divorce lawyer's desk, there was even more of a drastic reduction in trials and appeals as I learned first-hand that some fights simply did not make any economic sense.

Nevertheless, some trials are necessary. Much more importantly, though, the threat of trial greatly helps your negotiating position.

Although trials on the issue of the divorce itself were rare, I have had several trials on the issue for both strategic and non-strategic reasons. More on that shortly. When New York became a "no-fault State," trials on the grounds for divorce became extinct.

When a divorce action went to trial, it was the collateral issues of children, support, and property that became the focal points. These issues were also the subject of virtually all appellate matrimonial litigation.

Without those collateral issues resolved, your foreign divorce was merely your first stop on the judicial merry-go-round. You were bound to return to court in New York, assuming your one-sided divorce out-of-state was valid, to work out the real issues between you and your spouse. (Not surprisingly, in those instances there were often new spouses generating another kind of influence on the client.)

There were instances where the divorce was all the client wanted – situations where there were no children and where spousal support and property distribution were not in issue. These were not generally part of my practice.

But in the 1960s, probably at least in part because the State of New York realized it was losing revenue by having its residents go elsewhere in the first instance for their divorce, there was a relaxing of the grounds. "Cruel and inhuman treatment" and "abandonment" were the primary grounds added at that time. Later, there would be an expansion to two types of no-fault grounds for "conversion" of a legal separation (either from a judgment of separation or a written separation agreement signed within specific rules) after at least a year of living separate and apart. To top that off, there was no automatic conversion; rather, you had to sue your spouse in Court to obtain a judgment of divorce. In other words, you had to start a brand-new lawsuit to "convert" either the prior judgment or agreement of separation, and the plaintiff in the new action needed to prove that the parties lived separate and apart but also that he or she was in "substantial compliance" with the terms of the judgment or agreement of separation – with non-compliance serving as a defense to the later divorce action. Importantly, during the time you were legally separated (which must always be distinguished from just living apart, which I always called a simply an "estrangement" that has no legal impact), you are still married. That has some plusses and some minuses. You still qualified under your spouse's health insurance, but if you had a sexual relationship with a new partner, you and he/she were adulterers and, thus, technically criminals.

Of course, that led to considerable litigation and appellate rulings on what exactly "cruel and inhuman treatment" and "abandonment" were.

Suffice it to say, "cruel and inhuman treatment" was never viewed as being as abhorrent as the words suggest. "Cruel and inhuman treatment" was essentially "mean and rotten" (my words) acts or later just "bad stuff" (also my term), and it was determined that the proofs of misconduct had to show a higher level of severity when the marriage was more long-term. This means that some inappropriate conduct might be sufficient to entitle the victim to a divorce in a marriage of two or three years in length might, but the same misdeeds did not qualify for a divorce on cruelty grounds for a marriage of a decade or two.

"Abandonment" morphed from a spouse leaving the home and being away for at least a year to "constructive abandon-ment." "Constructive abandonment" means that the spouses are still in the same household – sometimes even in the same bed – but not having sexual relations. As I will describe later, there are defenses to even constructive abandonment.

During the times in which only fault grounds were available for divorce, the divorce was not *pro forma*. A plaintiff (the spouse who started the legal proceedings) must prove that the fault exists, and the defendant-spouse could, as the name implies, defend against the claims. A failure to prove the ground or grounds for fault divorce resulted in the plaintiff's case being dismissed and the parties remaining married.

Why would anyone want that to be the result of the divorce action after each side spent thousands, and sometimes tens of thousands, of dollars in legal fees?

The answer is money – almost always substantially more than the legal fees.

The Divorce Court as well as the Family Court had and has the power ("jurisdiction") to determine child custody and parenting issues even if a divorce is not granted. Similarly, these courts are also empowered to resolve support issues for the benefit of children and spouses where there is no matrimonial relief being granted.

However, what the Family Court cannot do – that is, what it is without the jurisdiction or authority to address – is grant a divorce itself or rule on the distribution of property. The so-called Divorce Court – a part of the "Supreme Court" in New York and a part of the "Superior Court" in New Jersey – can only divide the property of the marital estate only after divorce relief is granted. This means that if the Court hearing the divorce issues concluded that the divorce could not be appropriately granted, that Court was without the power to hear and rule upon the property division issues.

Furthermore, the state of the law before 1980 was such that a spouse guilty of a fault ground for divorce (adultery, cruel and inhuman treatment, or abandonment) was disqualified from receiving spousal support. While child support remained on the table, spousal support (then still called "alimony" in New York) would not be considered by the Court for a party who had committed the "fault."

Back then, both before and after the subsequent enactment of the Equitable Distribution Law in July of 1980 (and until there was later legislation allowing for complete no-fault divorce without any possible defense), if there were property issues that were not beneficial for one of the spouses to address, an option was to fight the divorce and keep the spouses legally married to each other. (Later changes to the law eliminated that strategy and severely limited the art of lawyering in these cases.)

Although counter-intuitive to a person involved in a divorce action, the fight-the-divorce option was a valuable strategic alternative for the divorce lawyer.

This is one instance where the knowledge, skills and experience of the divorce lawyer came into play. It was where true lawyering was involved; it was where there was room for negoti-ation – *you can have the divorce (i.e., I will not contest the grounds), if you make a concession to me on support, property settlement, or even custody and the child access schedule.*

You should also be aware that both before and after the 1960s change in the law, New York was and remained a "title State." What does that mean? The short answer: EVERYTHING.

Indeed, the Law involved in family cases was male-oriented, as was the world.

Going back to the caveman, the man was the hunter-gatherer out in the world while his spouse, the woman, stayed home and took care of the cave and the children.

Were a woman found to have committed adultery, she may well have been stoned to death. Were a man to have cheated on his partner, his friends would pat him on the back, congratulate him, and ask in which cave the new woman could be found.

As humans moved out of the caves, onto the farms, and even-tually, into the cities, society remained male-dominated.

This is the background for traditional family law, going back decades, if not centuries, with most marriages consisting of a working husband and a stay-at-home, child-raising wife. This was well before the notions of women's liberation and same-sex marriage. Again, traditionally, as the wage earner, the husband took title to the house and often maintained most of the bank accounts, and pensions were the property of the earner.

In other instances, a spouse (usually the husband) owned a business, and in an effort to shield the house from any possible business liability, the house was often put in the wife's name. This was not a rarity; in fact, my mother held title to the house I grew up in for this very reason. This immunized the family home from business debts.

So, what does this mean, or what did it mean in a "title State" like New York at that time?

Quite simply, it meant that if an asset were in a husband's name, he received that asset in the divorce free and clear of any interest of his wife, and if an asset were in a wife's name, she received that asset in the divorce free and clear of any interest of her husband.

If the family home was held in the sole name of the husband, he retained the house in the divorce. If that home were held in the sole name of the wife, she would continue to own it exclusively after the divorce. If it were owned in the joint names of the husband and wife, they would own it 50-50 after the divorce.

Other assets may represent a large portion of the marital estate (all of the assets of the husband and the wife). A business owned in the sole name of one spouse, whether that business was started before or during the marriage, would be determined to be the titleholder's asset, with the spouse getting no part of it in a divorce. In the hypothetical of my parents' divorce, it would have meant that Mom would get the house (with both their names on the mortgage) while Dad would have received all business assets and debt.

Similarly, retirement benefits earned by one spouse would be the sole and exclusive property of the husband/wife that earned those benefits, with the spouse having no claim to any of those benefits.

This was never very fair. One spouse could wind up homeless and penniless. Often, they did.

Laws eventually changed to prevent a woman from becoming a public charge. Mankind need not congratulate itself for this development as it was merely designed to have the husband support his wife rather than leaving it for society (i.e., the taxpayer) to provide such support.

On the other hand, an alimony award to the dependent spouse was usually for the rest of the recipient spouse's (usually the wife's) life unless she remarried, at which time alimony would terminate. Any post-divorce disability or retirement of the alimony payor did not impact the lifetime award of alimony.

This was the state of the law until July 19, 1980, when the Equitable Distribution Law went into effect. (I became a full-time divorce lawyer only two weeks before.)

New York was no longer a "title State" (albeit with plenty of litigation at both the trial and appellate levels concerning the difference between divorce cases starting before, on, or after the effective date).

First and foremost, it substituted equitable distribution in place of title, meaning that the Court is to determine what the property of the marriage is (which may include certain, but not all, appreciation of assets held by one party before the marriage), regardless of whose name appears on the title (the deed or other ownership instrument), and to distribute the property between the two spouses in an equitable, or fair, manner. This is distinguishable from a "community property" State wherein the Court divides property 50-50. Notably, California is a community property jurisdiction. While New York and New Jersey are "equitable distribution" states and are not mandated to distribute property equally between the spouses, there is often a 50-50 split of all marital property, especially where the marriage is one of a long duration; the longer the marriage, the better chance of a 50-50 division of assets.

Of course, there are also exceptions and a closely held business may be divided unevenly, as can every other aspect. The business is rarely divided equally and often in skewed percentages.

Equitable distribution, like community property, is based upon the theory that a marriage is "an economic partnership," a term coined by the appellate courts to explain the need for an "equitable" distribution of the assets of the parties.

There were certain exceptions to the "economic partnership"

rationale, which related to a spouse's "separate property." Separate property was the property that a spouse came into the marriage owning. Separate property also includes any property acquired by a spouse during the marriage by gift or inheritance – as long as the gift was not from the other spouse, as those gifts were considered marital property. Separate property also included any recovery for a personal injury (such as injuries in a car crash) sustained by a spouse.[1]

It was incumbent upon the spouse seeking to prove an asset was his or her separate property to prove the same as the law had a presumption that all of the property that a divorcing couple had was marital rather than separate property.

The classification of property issues was rife for litigation for years and, indeed, decades following 1980.

Indeed, property issues became a three-pronged analysis. First, a determination had to be made as to whether the particular asset was "marital," "separate" or "mixed" with mixed meaning partially separate and partially marital such as a business that a spouse owned at the time of the parties' wedding which grew and became more valuable during a marriage.

Then, there were considerations about how to deal with the accretion of value of a separate property asset. Different rules applied when the increase in value was the result of the active involvement of one or both spouses or whether the increase in value was due to passive market conditions over which neither party had any control. Were an asset to have appreciated during the marriage as a result of market conditions only (such as an increase in the value of a publicly traded stock), the appreciation

---

1. Interestingly, personal injury attorneys often added a second Plaintiff to their case when their injured client was married. That second Plaintiff had an independent claim for loss of consortium, meaning the injury had caused an interruption in the sex lives of the spouse. Thus, in some circumstances there were separate property interests of each spouse in the personal injury recovery.

was "passive," resulting in such an asset that one party brought into the marriage remaining separate property regardless of the increase (or decrease) in the value of the property. If the increase in the value was because of an addition to the house or an actively managed business, then the increase in value would be considered to be a marital asset, even if the underlying property was acquired by a spouse before the marriage. In that case, the original value was the separate property of the titleholder, while the increase in its value was a marital asset to be divided between the parties.

The second part of the property distribution process was to determine the value of the asset. Valuation is accomplished by one of two means: the parties agree as to the value of an asset (but with parties to a divorce action usually unable to agree if the sky were blue or what day of the week it was, this was a rarity); or an expert was retained to do a formal analysis to appraise the value of an asset. I can still remember that on literally the first day of law school more than 45 ago, my property law professor standing at the lectern, asking, *"How do you determine value?"* and when no one responded, he slammed his hand on that lecture while practically yelling at us, *"You Hire An Expert!!!"* Only an expert (sufficiently qualified to testify in court as to his or her expertise in evaluating that type of asset) can definitively provide a basis of value.

Unfortunately, no two experts agree on anything. This means that a divorce trial may have his and her experts, or there may be joint experts either agreed to by both sides or selected by the Court. Asset evaluation is, in many instances, more of an art than a science, depending on the type of asset. A bank account or a publicly traded stock does not require expert evaluation as those values are self-evident; and with those, the only questions would be on what date to evaluate the asset and the impact of any deposit or withdrawal to those types of assets during the marriage, as well as any other separate property considerations that may be existing.

The third prong is the distribution itself which occurs only after the classification of the property as something other than "separate" and only after it is evaluated. As noted, a marital asset is not always divided 50-50, but it often is so resolved.

A bank account or publicly traded asset is almost always – there are no absolutes in divorce law – subject to an equal division where a Court to decide the issue; and because of this, the parties usually agree to an equal distribution of this type of asset to avoid the litigation expense; alternatively, they may agree on an unequal distribution of such assets if part of a bigger picture of settling all property issues.

The marital home is similar in that it is typically an equal distribution but with another question becoming the date of the sale of the house, particularly when dependent children are continuing to reside in that home with one of the spouses. The Court is empowered to grant one spouse exclusive use and occupancy of an asset such as a house and to defer the sale of the asset (and division of the proceeds) to either a later date or until after the happening of a specific event such as the youngest child's graduation from high school.

Pensions and other retirement benefits of a spouse were a little more complicated, resulting in substantial litigation during the years immediately following the 1980 enactment of the Equitable Distribution Law. While there was substantial lawyering involved in the resolution of the pension distribution issue, that is no longer the situation as the caselaw resolved the matter. Now, it is largely math: whatever period of time existed between Spouse A starting to earn the retirement benefit was the sole property of that Spouse A without claim by Spouse B, the time between the marriage (the day they said "*I do*") to the earlier of the retirement date or the date a divorce action was formally commenced with the filing of a divorce summons in Court by one of the spouses (that day they said *"I don't"*) which is a 50-50 distribution, and finally, the period, if any, between the commencement of the divorce and the retirement date which would again be the sole property of that Spouse A without claim by Spouse B. This is commonly known as the *Majauskas* formula named for the litigants in a 1984 determination by New York's highest court.

The resulting division of the retirement benefit would either be a determination that one-half of the marital portion of the pension being paid to the non-titled spouse (with present values and tax considerations – all determined by a tax expert and/or actuary or possibly the pension plan administrator) or having a formula being employed so that a fraction of eventual periodic payment of retirement benefit (using the three pertinent time periods) being divided by the parties so that between the two spouses they are receiving 100% of each benefit check, almost always with the greater portion going to the employee spouse (unless the situation existed where the parties were already married when the benefit started, they were still married on the retirement date, and the divorce action was commenced at a later time in which instance there would be 50-50 division).

Unfortunately, the division of retirement assets between the spouses is even more complicated because the whole point of retirement benefits is to defer the tax bite of earned income from the time it was earned until some future time (usually when the spouses are in lower tax brackets). Because of tax considerations and, further, because ex-spouses are understandably distrusting of their exes to do right by the other at some future time, the sharing of the future benefit has to be guaranteed by a legal document called a Qualified Domestic Relations Order (or QDRO) which directs the retirement plan itself to perform the division as opposed to sending it all to Spouse A and expecting that he/she will honor the commitment to pay a specified percentage to

Spouse B. (Indeed, tax considerations such as capital gains are also matters which must be addressed in a fair settlement; and where there is a trial, expert testimony relative to tax consequences must be placed in evidence before the Judge.)

While the granting of the QDRO is one of the few *pro forma* acts of a Judge in a divorce action, the process is governed by the retirement plan administrator – with each plan having its own specific requirements. Given the tedious nature of complying with the demands of each plan administrator, divorce lawyers usually hire experts (actuaries) who only do QDRO preparation and retirement benefits appraisals for the simple reason that it is undeniably more cost-effective for the client to pay the expert than to pay the lawyer to go back and forth with each administrator.

This also allows the parties to divide a future asset without an immediate tax impact. Instead of the government receiving its cut on the earned income at the time of the divorce, the tax burden to each spouse remains deferred to the actual receipt of funds with the use of a QDRO. But it should never be forgotten that the retirement benefit is paid for income already earned and that there will be an income tax paid by each spouse on the retirement benefit that he/she receives in the future, regardless of which spouse initially earned the money.

The distribution of a spouse's interest in a business is an even more complicated issue. Perhaps the following actual situation – a case study, if you will – will illustrate the complexities. I represented a wife whose husband was a part owner of a large and successful automobile franchise. Before the parties married, the husband had a small ownership interest in the dealership where he was employed. During the marriage, he received another portion of the dealership as a gift from his father, and he purchased another portion from his uncle. The purchased portion of his interest was a marital asset. But that did not end the analysis because the dealership franchise became very successful during the course of the marriage largely due to the active involvement of the husband and those under his employ, so successful that the franchise more than doubled in value by the time the divorce action started. That appreciation in the value of the entire dealership, to both the separate and the marital portions of the business, was in and of itself marital property to which my client was entitled to her participation interest.

This necessitated that my client and I hire a business appraiser and/or forensic accountant to provide a step-by-step analysis of what was marital and what was separate, as well as to determine the value of the during-the-marriage appreciation of the husband's premarital interest, as well as such appreciation of the gifted portion, and the entire value of the purchased portion of the property.

Moreover, while the wife's side had her expert to maximize these values, the husband and his lawyer hired their own expert to minimize those values.

This ultimately resulted in a five-week trial costing each spouse over $100,000 in legal fees not to mention the experts' fees, a lengthy written decision by the trial judge, and ultimately (with other counsel) an appeal.

In addition to the aforementioned assets, any other thing of value owned by the parties is available for equitable distribution. Some assets are so minimal in value that the process of a judicial distribution would greatly outweigh the asset itself making it pointless to explore. Art collections and the like may be valuable enough that experts will be needed.

Furniture and furnishings of a home that is being sold should be divided between the parties themselves by taking turns off of a list of the items. No lawyer should be required to do this for the parties; the costs of lawyers are such that the legal expense would dwarf the value of these assets. As I previously referenced in my

Psychology Today article, it makes no sense to spend $5,000 in legal fees over a $1,000 television set – even if you ultimately "win" on this issue, you would be better off buying a new one with enhanced technology that would be substantially less costly. Indeed, simply walking away from such an item is the alternative.

The same analysis, including a separate versus marital determination, is also applied to each debt of the parties as the Court must "equitably distribute" the marital debts of the parties.

There is another issue with property distribution. That is the question of the pets. As a very young divorce attorney, I used to tell clients that they needed to work out the issue of who gets the dog because I did not know what standard to apply to pets: Were we to equitably distribute the dog or were we to consider the best interests of the dog? In later years, two things happened: First, people started to litigate the pet issue. Initially, the pet was determined to be another asset to be distributed as property in a divorce action. Only in very recent years did that caselaw evolve to a point where the pet's well-being was a factor in with whom the pet would live. Second, I appeared before a Judge who was a pet lover (ultimately retiring from the Bench to run an animal rescue facility). In conference with this Judge, we advised the Court that the parties agreed that each spouse would keep one of the dogs. *"Oh no, you won't!"* demanded the Judge, *"Those dogs need each other!"*

Even though the case law had yet to change, the Judge demanded certain things. This was a lesson not merely about pets but about knowing who your Judge is and what that Judge requires.

The enactment of the Equitable Distribution Law, although its title would suggest that it was only about property distribution, had various other matters included in it.

The concept of alimony was changed dramatically. Indeed, the word itself, "alimony," was eliminated from the lexicon in New York (it remains in New Jersey) and replaced with the word "maintenance" or the term "spousal maintenance" or "spousal support" to distinguish it from child support. The "disqualification" from maintenance for a spouse "guilty" of a marital fault fortunately became no more. Further, maintenance can now be durational, meaning that it was not necessarily intended to last for the lifetime of the recipient as had been the old law where there was either no alimony or lifetime alimony and nothing in between.

In later years, many States (among them my jurisdictions of New York and New Jersey) instituted Guidelines for alimony/maintenance in the form of formulae for determining both amount and duration, which were separate from the child support Guidelines that had already been in place to determine the amount of child support to be paid based on the income of the respective parties and other factors. The alimony/maintenance formula was used first, with the child support formula being secondarily applied, with the alimony received considered to be income to the recipient spouse (and alimony paid as a reduction in income to the paying spouse) when the child support formula is applied.

More recently, the Federal tax laws changed. Up until most recently, alimony/spousal maintenance was a taxable event. The paying spouse obtained a deduction from his/her income; and the recipient spouse was required to recognize this alimony support, as distinguished for child support, taxable income. A good rule of thumb is that the government never loses; where there is a payment deductible to one party, someone else (the recipient spouse) is required to claim the income on the recipient's tax return and to pay the taxes thereon.

But, as noted, this is no longer the case. Without addressing politics – and that would be a whole separate undertaking – the tax laws no longer provide for alimony to be deductible to the payor and taxable to the payee. Among the reasons why is that the alimony payor is ordinarily in a higher tax bracket than the recipient. Again, the government never loses; there are more taxes to be paid by the person in the higher bracket.

Interestingly, the Guidelines imposed in most/all States for determining a calculation for an amount of alimony to be paid were all formulated *before* the change in the tax laws regarding deductibility. Yet once the tax laws changed, no State altered its Guidelines. This means when representing a spousal support payor, any divorce attorney worth his or her salt must go to the trouble of doing the Guidelines calculations (not a big deal, but required), calculating what the tax impact would have been had the Guidelines amount been deductible to the payor and taxable to the recipient spouse (hire an accountant for this as this is an area rife for malpractice) and then argue to the Judge on trial (and to the other side in negotiations) that there needs to be a "deviation" (a statutory term of art) from the Guidelines primarily on this modification of the tax laws.

As you will see, my personal preference has always been for more lawyering and negotiation to determine issues in a divorce rather than simply imposing a mathematical formula.

But don't expect the Court to do this for you. Anything that you want the Judge to consider must be spelled out with specifics, and that goes double for tax considerations. The Court will not "do the math." Indeed, for the Court to perform a deviation from the support guidelines, it must state what the support would have been using the guidelines formula and then set forth its reasons for such deviation. The lawyer must put all this before the Judge because that is the only way there will be a chance of deviation. Even were a Judge to sign off on a deviation from the support Guidelines without the requisite recitation of the mathematical reasons, the Clerk would be required to "bounce" the final papers as not being consistent with statutory requirements. In other words, even a signed Judgment of Divorce could not be entered by the Clerk – and thus not considered "final" for any purpose, including death or remarriage. Without the required language and the "doing of the math," the entire divorce proceedings would have been an exercise in futility.

The 1980 legislative change also removed marital fault as a factor in alimony determinations, and it also removed marital fault in property division determinations. Except in cases where the marital misconduct was "egregious." But what is "egregious?" New York decisional law has cited a New Jersey case which gave as an example of this type of really bad misconduct that could be considered by a Court as an instance where one spouse had "put out a hit" on the life of the other.

That's really bad.

Adultery is not egregious; nor is transmitting a sexually transmitted disease to your spouse. That's not "bad enough" to constitute egregious misconduct under the law. Judges may have been thinking that either 1) if adultery is egregious, then we will have to consider this in all divorces (with more evidence, longer trials, and more work for the judge) or even 2) if adultery is egregious, that may become a factor in *my* divorce.

I have surmised that the intentional transmission of AIDS may well be egregious; but then again, with recent medical breakthroughs, maybe it's not as egregious as I had originally considered. In any event, that issue has not reached the reported judicial decisions; so, we just don't know if giving your spouse AIDS would constitute egregious misconduct in a divorce setting.

In addition to property and maintenance matters, the Equitable Distribution Law also went on to include provisions for life insurance when necessary to ensure that the maintenance and child support would be paid upon the demise of the payor spouse. This then new law also provided for circumstances in which modification of support would be appropriate.

The statutory law then changed again around 2010, when New York added "irretrievable breakdown of the marriage" as a ground for divorce. This made New York the 50th State to recognize truly no-fault divorce and what is known in most other jurisdictions as "irreconcilable differences;" but don't use that term in the New York courts. Nevertheless, there is absolutely no difference between marriages that are irreconcilable and those that are irretrievably broken.

Personally, I never liked the no-fault grounds, but that is from the perspective of a trial lawyer. Not only do some people not want to be divorced – and I could name several to whom this applies, both professionally and personally – but, as noted, the Court is not empowered to effectuate a distribution of marital property unless and until a divorce is determined to be awarded. (However, issues of support and child custody can be determined regardless of whether or not there is a termination of the marriage.)

In the past, but unfortunately not now, the marital fault grounds trial was another implement in the divorce lawyer's toolkit in negotiating for his/her client. Essentially saying, *"Okay, if you don't like our proposal on property distribution, then we don't agree to the divorce; and when we win on trial, there won't be ANY property distribution."* I have successfully negotiated better resolutions for my clients; I have successfully tried grounds trials where the parties remained married at the end of the litigation.

Indeed, this book is filled with War Stories (which is the real reason it has been written). One such story occurred at the beginning of my legal career. I recall a situation in a pre-equitable distribution case where, after a six-week trial, the Judge ruled essentially, *A pox on both your houses; neither one of you gets a divorce.* This, of course, led to an appeal by both spouses. In a conference in the Appellate Division before argument, the wise old Judge looked at me and my client, then looked at the wife's counsel and his client before returning to me saying, *"How much is your client willing to pay to get rid of this cancer?"* After years of litigation, the case then settled in 15 minutes; and the parties were divorced shortly thereafter.

Another War Story: I represented a man who did not want his property to be divided between him and his wife. He did not love her; and she certainly wanted nothing to do with him. She started a divorce action based upon constructive abandonment, claiming that he refused to have sex with her. We defended and ultimately went to trial. The trial testimony was such that she had made no sexual advances towards her husband and thus had not been abandoned by him. What the testimony further revealed was that my client had regularly, at least once or twice each week, made both verbal and physical overtures to his wife to engage in sexual relations with her, but that she had, on each occasion, thwarted those overtures. While my client, the husband, may well have had a cause of action for divorce based upon constructive aban-donment, we argued that we were not seeking a divorce; never-theless, she was not entitled to a divorce against him. After a trial in which each side presented testimony of "the facts," we won; and the case was "dismissed with prejudice" which meant that the wife could no longer get a divorce against the husband at any time in the future based upon actions (or inactions) occurring before the first trial. Years later, the same client came back to me and presented me with a new summons for divorce (brought by another lawyer representing his wife). The parties had not recon-ciled, had not lived together, nor done much of anything with the other in all that time. While we could have successfully defended the second action, my client was neither interested in paying me for another trial nor in staying married to this woman. Fortu-nately, the woman wanted out of the marriage more on the second go-round than she did the first time. With the first dismissal, however, I was able to negotiate a *"you go your way and I go mine"* divorce settlement, completely avoiding contested proceedings over property distribution.

Yet Another War Story: On another occasion, my client truly loved his wife. He refused to consent to his wife divorcing him; and he refused to consent to her having custody of the children, who were teenage girls who wanted to live with their mom. There was nothing that I could say that would convince this man to consent to the divorce; if possible, there was even less I could do to get him to agree to joint custody legal custody of his daughters.

So, we had the trial on the grounds of constructive abandonment (*"my spouse stopped having sexual intercourse with me for more than a year despite my repeated requests for a resumption of such relations"*) and because of cruel and inhuman treatment. The wife alleged that my client refused to have sexual intercourse (and that term is used because that is what the law requires to be alleged and proven as refused, as opposed to the vague term of marital relations or sexual relations) with her for the past six years, and because *"he was mean and rotten to me"* (again, my words).

Our defense: What do you mean six years? We haven't had sex with her in ten years because we (my client, the husband) were (was) impotent. And, even if we did the bad things you claim we did, it was not enough to constitute cruelty in this long-term 20-year marriage as the law provided that the longer the marriage, the more harsh the conduct necessary to constitute "cruel and inhuman treatment" – in other words, something that was considered to be sufficiently cruel to terminate a three-year marriage might not be cruel enough to end a 20-year marriage. What the wife claimed to be cruelty on the part of the husband was *"not bad enough"* to support a divorce finding. We, of course, denied that my client had done anything improper in his marriage, but he retained the same personality that served him as a teenager when he crossed the Berlin Wall.

I kid you not: I tried this case without the benefit of expert testimony as to my client's impotence. Instead, I tried this case before an Irish Catholic Judge and brought into Court every neighbor to whom the wife had told that her husband could not obtain an erection. But isn't the testimony of someone telling the Court what another person said considered to be hearsay and not admissible evidence? Actually, the hearsay rule (and every person has heard about hearsay on television and in the movies), there are many exceptions to the rule prohibiting hearsay, one of which is when the party being quoted makes a declaration against his/her own interests. The admission by this wife that her husband was impotent was a declaration against her own interests for seeking a divorce based upon sexual abandonment.

The result: We won on the constructive abandonment grounds, but alas, we lost on cruelty. Not unexpectedly, we also lost custody of the two teenage daughters who wanted to live with their mother.

Children do not get to make the choice of which parent they get to live with. The younger the child, the less say they have. But as they age, the children get input; and an independent attorney is often appointed for them. They used to be called Law Guardians and now are simply called Attorneys for the Child(ren). Sometimes, when the children have differing concerns separate attorneys for each child are appointed. Before New York's Family Court, where parties are often before the Court without their own lawyer (and it is not unusual for neither party to have a private lawyer), the Judge will appoint an Attorney for the Child to get the views of the child expressed on the record. In less recent times, the Attorney for the Child (AFC) would express his or her judgment instead of mirroring the client/child; still, this occurs with younger children. (AFCs also express their own opinions. While it is appropriate for an AFC to act so, the attorney for a parent should properly object to the voicing of an AFC opinion when the child is so young as not to have his or her own voice heard.)

Having that background, the opinion of a teenager from age 14 on becomes more dispositive until the age of 18 when the Court loses jurisdiction (the power to decide) issues of custody and visitation even though consideration by the Court of the child support obligation may extend to age 21 or beyond. As an example (a war story within a war story, if you will), I was representing the mother of a sixteen-year-old before the Family Court. Just before the lunch break, the boy testified before the Judge, *"If you make me live with my mother, I'm gonna run away again."* I suggested that my client think long and hard over the next hour about what she wanted to do, as the Judge was unlikely to ignore such a remark. My client assured me that she would do so. An hour later, I returned to Court for the afternoon session. My client never came back to Court, never called me again, nor responded to any inquiry from my office, and, needless to say, did not pay the balance of her bill to me.

Returning to my Berlin Wall crosser, the teenage daughters, 15 and 17, adored their mother. There was testimony that it was the mother who was more involved in the lives of the girls, addressing their educational, social, and all of their other needs, as well as additional testimony that she was a well-respected member of the community. Further, her appearance and self-assured manner before the Court were in sharp contrast to that of my client, whose personality had not markedly changed since he had crossed the Wall as a youth. Quite frankly, the wife, in this case, was so wonderful that when testimony was elicited, she revealed, in addition to everything else, that she was also a deacon in the local church; this immediately prompted me to walk up to the lectern from where her lawyer was doing the questioning and whisper in his ear, *"The horse is dead."*

As my client only cared about keeping his wife and kids, following the unfavorable determinate on grounds for divorce and residential custody of the children, we quickly agreed to a visitation/parenting schedule and to support and distribution. This gentleman could have elected to appeal the divorce decision and/or the custody ruling (which I advised against), but he was wise enough to accept reality and move on.

This husband could have received joint legal custody of the girls and a pain-free divorce. But he steadfastly insisted that he would not "give" his wife either the divorce or residential custody of their daughters.

Before you ask, he was fully advised by me before the trial about the costs – legal, emotional, and financial – of the trial process. It was his divorce; I was merely the lawyer. Being a divorce lawyer is akin to being hired as a ship captain: I am employed to get the ship from Point A to Point B; and I explain where the rough waters exist and steer the ship. But the client owns the boat, decides what we are hauling, and ultimately determines whether Point B is a viable destination even when the captain offers alternatives. This client's costs had substantially escalated because of his unreasonable position requiring a trial.

The lack of a no-fault divorce ground at the time was great for the lawyer as it gave me another tool in the shed to use to advance my client's position, whether it was at trial or in negotiations – and my *client's position* is always my primary obligation. It was not so great for the litigants as it forced a trial that cost each party days and thousands of dollars to end the marriage that had no business surviving. The divorce process itself clouds the waters and the vision of the litigant to the extent that rational decision-making, often is obscured by the emotion that is behind it.

So now, the divorce lawyer has a lot on his/her plate in terms of what to do.

1. Do we sue on "irretrievable breakdown" grounds or some other ground that remains viable? I always have added a second ground, even if it is only for a divorce based upon "constructive abandonment" when there are unresolved support and property distribution issues. Why do I do this? Experience. New York law provides that the irretrievable breakdown ground for divorce is not available upon default (meaning the other party does not show up on the case) unless all financial and custodial issues have been resolved.

War story: I had a client whose wife was in Africa. With great difficulty, we had her personally served with process in Africa, but we only sought the divorce only on the grounds of irretrievable breakdown. The statute providing for this ground makes the matrimonial relief unavailable when the defendant-spouse fails to appear, either individually or through counsel. This led to motion practice for which I could not morally charge my client and added months to the process. From that point forward, I remembered to never start litigation without including at least one fault ground; it could always be withdrawn at a later time (such as when the other side formally appears in the case or in some way challenges the divorce litigation).

2. What are the other issues to be considered?

a. Child custody and visitation, if applicable.

b. Child support, if the children are under 21, or are 22 (or older) and still in school (and if you want child support past age 21, you must specifically ask for that in the Summons or the pleadings). Do you want to accept the amount of support that the Child Support Guidelines would call for, or do you want to "opt-out" and select a higher or a lower amount?

c. College, depending on if there is a child or are children and the ages of each child. Is the child ready for college? (One of my cases decided on appeal stood for the principle that college for a fifteen-year-old was too speculative for a trial court to address and that the issue should have "awaited a more appropriate time" for consideration.) Do you want to address college for younger children now or defer the issue until the child is ready? Do you want the parties to start contributing now towards a college fund such as a 529 account (particularly, when they started to do so before the parties sought legal representation in "happier times")? [This is something that you would not get from a Court which lacked the power to grant such relief, but which could be obtained through negotiations.] Do you want to obligate the parties to pay for any college or do you want to cap responsibility at the State College (the SUNY system in New York, Rutgers in New Jersey) rate existing at that time? Do you want to give the parent paying support a credit against child support for the amount that he/she is paying for room and board at college?

War Story: I was representing a childhood friend who went through both school and summer camp with me. I did not hide my background from the other side. During negotiations, we steadfastly insisted upon the college obligation being limited to what the college costs would be if the child were then attending the most expensive school in the State University of New York (SUNY) system. When Mom's lawyer asked me why, I responded that there was no doubt that my client would contribute more money if the child got into Harvard, but that we would not have my client contractually bound to pay for Boston University. The other lawyer responded that the problem in the case was that I "loved" my client. I assured this attorney that I had previously and would continue in the future to advance this position for any client and not merely because of the personal connection.

d. Is there going to be spousal maintenance? And if so, for what duration and in what amount? Do you want to accept the amount and duration of maintenance that the Maintenance (or

Alimony) Guidelines would call for or do you want to "opt-out" of the Guidelines, and select a higher or a lower amount? Alternatively, one spouse could buy out the other's right to alimony / maintenance.

Personal War Story: At the time of my own divorce in the State of New Jersey, I was looking at long-term, if not permanent (i.e., forever) alimony. The only marching order I gave to my lawyer during the divorce (and yes, I had my lawyer, because (i) I remembered Lincoln's admonishment about the lawyer representing himself having a fool for a client, and (ii) the emotions I was feeling -- not to mention the venom -- made detached lawyering an impossibility) was that *I want to be able to retire SOMEDAY."* The process was long and drawn out; and we eventually saw a second mediator (because, as my lawyer put it, *"Your wife won't agree to anything unless she hears it from a Judge,"* thus necessitating the discharge of the lawyer-mediator and his replacement with a retired judge-mediator) who suggested the buy-out of alimony. Negotiations continued with my wife receiving almost all of the proceeds of the sale of our house (less enough for me with which to pay my legal fees), plus annual payments for six years, with various calculations being done because by that point the tax deductibility of alimony was history, and other calculations for a prepayment discount. This was essentially a front-loaded payment of what would likely have been a lifetime obligation in smaller monthly amounts. This was a risk for me because I would have "lost" (i.e., paid more than necessary) had my wife remarried, or either of us died before the end of the six years. But it gave me the finality that I craved. Now, more than a dozen years after the divorce, I am in the process of retiring, having not paid my ex anything in several years and knowing I will never have to pay her again. Further, my ex is happy because she is rid of me, received a lot more money upfront from the house and during the first six years than she would have otherwise gotten, and did not have to worry about whether she would be receiving payments from me as the years went on. Thus, it was beneficial to each of us to settle "creatively," apart from what a straight application of the law in terms of spousal support and property distribution.

e. What is the marital property?

(i) Are there assets that are not marital property which are denominated as "separate property" (such as premarital assets, property acquired after a divorce has formally been commenced in Court, inherited property or property received as a gift from someone other than the spouse, and assets acquired with separate property assets)? Are there assets that were separate property but appreciated in value during the marriage? And if there was an appreciation to any such asset, was the reason for the appreciation to each such asset the result of purely market conditions (such as increases in the value of a portfolio of publicly traded stock), or was the reason for the appreciation because of the direct or indirect contribution of the spouse that did not have the separate property asset (such as improvements to separate property real estate during the marriage, or the direct contribution of one spouse's to the others premarital business or the spouse's services as a homemaker/parent to allow the party having the premarital business to increase its value? In other words, was the appreciation "active" or passive?" If purely market conditions, the other spouse is not entitled to the owner's appreciated asset; but if otherwise, that other spouse may be entitled to a piece of the appreciation of the asset. What percentage of the appreciation, if any, is the right amount because it will be something less, perhaps far less, than half?

(ii) Are there bank accounts and/or stock portfolios to be evaluated and divided? Is there a capital gains issue at hand? (Again, expert tax advice is necessary.)

(iii) Has either spouse or both spouses have any retirement

benefit? Pensions, 401-ks, and the like are typically divided evenly to the extent that they are marital; and there are formulae to determine what percentage of the retirement benefit is marital and what is separate.

(iv) What is the extent of the real estate of the parties?

(v) Is there a business or businesses to be evaluated and divided?

(vi) Are there any valuation issues for the various assets, and what experts are needed to submit reports or testify in Court? Unless the parties agree upon value (typically with a publicly traded stock or a bank account), *only an expert can determine value.* Might it be a good idea to stipulate or agree to values for certain assets? Sometimes, an asset is not worth what it would cost to have it professionally valued for the case. Do the parties want to agree upon a joint expert that would save the parties the expense of each of them having his/her own hired gun on the issue of valuation? Sometimes, it is wise to have your own, particularly when the asset is both valuable and the parties are far apart, and sometimes, it is the most cost-effective alternative to have a joint expert that the parties (with the help of their lawyers) can agree upon.

(vii) What about health insurance? Under Federal law, an insurer is not required to continue to provide for an employee's spouse upon the formal dissolution of the marriage (that is, the granting of the final judgment of divorce) and may offer that spouse continued coverage under COBRA which will not be free to the newly divorced ex-spouse of the employee. Consideration of health insurance costs following the divorce may be important on the amount of maintenance/alimony to be paid, or whether the working spouse may be required to provide a separate policy of health insurance for the other for a specified time. Or might it be prudent to just have the parties be legally separated and not divorced yet so that the health insurance coverage continues unchanged? Does your client want this, or do they oppose it? Even if financially advantageous, the spouse married to the employee may still want the divorce so badly that he/she doesn't care about the cost of health insurance. It is, nevertheless, the attorney's job to make clear the options and the consequences of such a decision, even though it is the client's ultimate determination what to do. In such cases, it is always advisable to make those options known to the client in writing or email so that later, when the client is looking for someone to blame for his/her own decision, there will be a paper trail establishing that it is not the lawyer. The title of this book is not BLAME BLOOM for nothing. And another thing: The old no-fault conversion divorce is still on the books, and either spouse may sue the other for the conversion divorce as early as one year after the parties live separate and apart following the granting of a judgment of separation or the signing of a separation agreement. One year goes by really fast, particularly if you are no longer sharing a home with your estranged spouse! It is the time before the physical separation that seems to stand still when the marriage is far less than ideal.

(viii) If there are ongoing obligations of a spouse, such as spousal or child support, college, or payouts over time of an interest in an asset, there must be security for the payments in the event that the paying spouse dies. Usually, that security is in the form of life insurance. However, in my own case, I was pushing 300 pounds when I finally ran away from home (separated), and I was literally uninsurable. It was not that the cost of the premiums was exorbitant; it was that no insurance carrier would issue a policy on my life at all. Fortunately, I am now considerably lighter. But more importantly, I was able to anticipate the request and had an alternative: the half of my retirement that she was not getting (and that I was not yet utilizing) was provided as security for my financial settlement, where the payments extended over several years.

(ix) Should the monied spouse contribute to the legal fees of the other spouse? And to what extent? This is something the Court has the power to grant and thus should be considered when negotiating towards a settlement.

(x) Other than the security issue, what provision is to be made for the "what if" scenario where the obligated spouse does not meet those obligations? When my client is the spouse receiving ongoing payments, I always insist that there be a "counsel fees in the event of a default" clause in the agreement.

(xi) And, finally, what would happen if the paying spouse declared bankruptcy? Child support and spousal maintenance are non-dischargeable obligations, which means that if the paying spouse declared bankruptcy, the obligated spouse would continue to be required to pay all such past, present, and future support. However, property distribution is dischargeable in bankruptcy, and without an agreement providing that a property distribution payment was to survive bankruptcy, it would be dischargeable in the bankruptcy. It is thus regular practice to insist upon survival language. Still, it has been remarkable to see how many attorneys simply forget to have this essential language added to protect his/her clients. Indeed, it is malpractice to not include survival language when your client is to receive future payments in a property settlement. (A completely different issue is whether the non-discharge of a property settlement is consistent with federal bankruptcy law. To my knowledge, this question of discharge has never been raised before, let alone decided by a Federal Bankruptcy or Appellate Court.)

3. There are also more subtle things to consider.

a. Do you want to start an action immediately or try to negotiate?

b. Do you want your client to be the Plaintiff or the Defendant in litigation? While this distinction is not truly relevant to the ultimate determinations from a legal standpoint, as the law is the same in either case, one has to consider whether the client wants to go first should the case ultimately go to trial. At trial, Plaintiff goes first. Can he or she withstand getting up to give sworn testimony; might it be more advisable to allow the other side to be the Plaintiff?

c. We divorce lawyers must also look not just at the two clients, but at opposing counsel as well. Is the other lawyer up for a trial? War story: I was hired as a lawyer for a Defendant, where the Plaintiff was represented by one of the very few lawyers in the field I could describe as a friend. To say the least, I knew him very well, and I knew that when a Judge said to him, *"Call your first witness,"* the guy would fold like the proverbial cheap suit. My duty was with the client; and I advised him to give me some leeway with the case because of this particular lawyer's fear of trial. My client agreed; and we settled in the Court House for a much better deal than had been offered before our trial date (and the offer had already been made better for my client as the trial date edged closer). As I have said to many people over many years, I don't do this work to make friends; I do it to protect my clients and to allow them to get on with their lives in the most advantageous circumstances possible.

d. In which Court do you want to bring suit, and in which county? In New York, only the Supreme Court (contrary to the United States Supreme Court or the New Jersey Supreme Court, which are the highest appellate courts, the New York Supreme Court is a trial-level court with a branch in each of the State's counties) may hear a divorce action. However, other family matters, such as child custody and visitation/parenting time, child and spousal support, paternity proceedings, and child abuse and neglect proceedings, may be brought in the Family Court, and adoptions can be brought in either the Family Court or the Surrogate's Court (with one in each county). In New Jersey, the trial level court is the Superior Court, with one in each county, with divorces in the Dissolution Part and non-divorce proceedings in the Non-Dissolution Part. The determination of which Court is to hear the case is a matter of "jurisdiction" and is defined in the statutes of each State based on residency and duration of that residency. Similarly, there may be a jurisdictional issue in a choice of suing in one of two or more States. Unless the parties have homes in different States or they have been living separately in different States for at least a year (or two), the jurisdictional issue of choice of State will be relatively straightforward. The question of which County to bring suit is one of "venue." The choice is made by the Plaintiff, the spouse that is starting the divorce action (unless the venue selected is totally inappropriate within the statutes of the State involved, in which case a demand for a venue change will be available). Venue in a matrimonial case is most often in one of the counties in which a party resides. Although not a factor in the choice of venue, a consideration may be the relative convenience of the lawyers and the inconvenience of the other party. An advantage to being the "Plaintiff" when the parties reside in separate Counties is that the Plaintiff chooses the venue, a choice that cannot be challenged unless the Plaintiff chooses a completely unrelated venue.

e. Does the client have any special needs that need to be addressed? Part of the lawyer's analysis about the duration of spousal maintenance (as well as child support) is whether the recipient spouse, often a stay-at-home mother, is expected to rejoin the workforce and what training over how long a time will be required (as well as the cost of such training), together with the earnings potential of that spouse once working again.

4. Is there a need for immediacy? Does the client need to get into Court fast because of any number of matters? Is there domestic violence? Is the client's spouse threatening to abscond with the child? Is the spouse dissipating marital assets? Is my client pregnant with someone else's baby (which has happened

with my clients on more than one occasion), or has another personal interest in moving on with his/her life? This is just the tip of the iceberg. Each divorce litigant is different with differing needs. Each divorce lawyer is different. Each matrimonial Judge has a different perspective formed from his/her own experience. Divorce is not a "one size fits all" determination, which is usually the default position of a lawyer who does not devote his/her entire practice to matrimonial matters.

5. If there is a pending case at the time of settlement, do the parties want to discontinue the case in a large, busy County to refile in another County elsewhere in the State of New York to avoid delay in the Court's processing of the divorce? On one occasion during the Covid-19 pandemic, one of my cases in Manhattan (New York County) settled. Because of the volume of pending divorce actions in the Manhattan Court, as well as other delays associated with the pandemic, my adversary suggested to me that we withdraw the Manhattan matter where my client was the Plaintiff and allow the other side to refile in Jefferson County. After discovering that the county seat in Jefferson County was Watertown, New York (roughly another hour of driving in good weather north of Syracuse) and after obtaining the assurance that neither my client nor I would ever have to set foot in Jefferson County, we agreed. What otherwise would have taken eighteen months or more to process the divorce in the then-pending New York County was accomplished in only three days up in Watertown for an additional cost of only a couple of hundred dollars, constituting a duplication of filing fees.

6. Finally, is the Judge a former practicing divorce attorney; or did the Judge have experience in another area of the law, having neither the knowledge nor the experience to delve into this area? As the Matrimonial Parts (those Judges handling only divorce and family law matters) are usually the busiest with the most work, the assignment of a Judge to this Part is often viewed by

the Judge as a punishment or a place for newly appointed Judges to start. Very rare is the case where the Judge had been a matrimonial attorney and wanted a Matrimonial Part assignment, although it is not unheard of for a former matrimonial practitioner to request assignment to the Family Part. Those are the Judges to whom I loved having my cases assigned.

But, forgetting those for a moment, what type of novice divorce Judge do you have?

a. Does the Judge want to work or want to learn? That is the second-best situation, as it gives the lawyer an opportunity to influence the judge in terms of that Judge's handling of this and all future cases.

b. Does the Judge truly want to help the litigants settle and get on with their lives? Surprisingly, there are very few who take a hands-on approach to settling cases early in the process before each side spends tens of thousands of dollars on legal fees. However, some want to move their calendars not simply for accolades in the number of cases they can complete but because of the finality it brings the litigants. It is a pleasure to practice before those members of the Judiciary. A Judge who does not want to try to reach a settlement and is hell-bent on going forward misses the opportunity to help the litigants while streamlining his or her own calendar. An example of this is the case where I represented the wife of the owner of most of a car dealership. The case had been assigned to a Judge that worked hard to settle all of his cases and that had been ruling in my client's favor during those occasions when he was forced to decide an issue. The husband hired a new lawyer during the course of the litigation. The new lawyer, an expert in the field, may well have been retained specifically because of his friendship with our case's Judge. This fact resulted in the recusal of the Judge (more on recusal later) and the reassignment of the matter to another Judge who made no effort whatsoever to have the parties reach a negotiated resolution of the issues, thus causing all of us to endure a five-week trial. The failure of this second Judge to knock heads towards a settlement cost the Judge a five-week backlog on her calendar, as well as costing the litigants tens of thousands each of additional legal fees.

c. Then there are the Judges who refuse to admit what they don't know and won't go out of their way to develop the special temperament needed for the Family Parts of the Court. Unfortunately, over a career spanning over four decades, that has been a majority of the Judges who are new to family law.

Quite simply, there is a lot to think about when you want to get divorced or when you are a lawyer meeting with a potential new client.

———

"WHAT ABOUT JURIES?" I am often asked. *"What does the jury decide?"*

The short answer is: NOTHING.

A jury may decide questions of law. Questions of equity in a court proceeding are issues for a Judge to decide.

The only legal issue in a divorce case is whether a party has proven a case for divorce. Every other matter in a divorce proceeding is a question of equity. Child custody and visitation, spousal and child support, the distribution of property, life insurance, health insurance, legal fees, and anything other than the marital relief itself – that is, whether there is a divorce or not – are equitable issues not within the purview of a jury.

With only the question of whether a divorce was to be granted properly before a jury, there was little cause for having a jury at all. Now, with divorce being available entirely in a no-fault setting where there is no defense whatsoever to the action for divorce, there is seldom a jury in a divorce case. The only exception would be in instances where one spouse seeks a monetary recovery for injuries sustained in domestic violence at the hand of the other. That would be just like any other typical tort claim such as an automobile accident or such as an assault and battery claim (committed by a non-spouse).

Before the no-fault divorce was enacted in New York, one could fight the divorce because no property division issues could be decided without the granting of a divorce. In those instances, a jury could have been called upon to decide the issue of the divorce and only the issue of the divorce.

Judges frowned upon juries hearing such an issue; and the lawyer was unlikely to go against a Judge's wishes.

Only once, in a non-divorce action, was I called upon to pick a jury. Frankly, jury selection is an art and not a science; it was not a good thing for me. After the jury's determination in the other party's favor, I have always said of juries, *"You get what you pay for!"*

Judges don't like juries because juries increase the Judge's workload, having to make sure that a certain decorum is maintained in the courtroom and mandating the issuance by the judge of specific instructions on the application of the law to the facts. With a jury, the Judge must also issue Jury Instructions before jury deliberation; and formulating the Instructions further adds to the Judge's workload.

Judges also like to say to lawyers, when the lawyer gives a particularly emotional appeal, *"There's no jury here, counselor."* This, of course, means that the Judge wants the lawyer to move on. I have heard that one on far more than one occasion.

CHAPTER 4
THE APPRENTICE
(NO, NOT THAT ONE!)

As I said, my second job as a real attorney was in a high-conflict divorce practice. I worked for the late Ira Richard Bennett.

I was the second attorney in a two-man law firm handling only family law cases in Manhattan and surrounding counties in New York. I learned more working with Ira than I had ever learned before.

I had a mentor. For the first time in my life, I had someone show me the ropes and introduce me to people. I had someone with whom to bounce ideas; and I had someone who took my suggestions seriously. Sometimes he accepted them; and sometimes he rejected them. But the ideas were always considered.

But for my dedicatees each being the special people that they are, this book could well have been dedicated to my mentor. Thank you, Ira.

Not only did I have an entirely family law caseload, but I was given room for creativity to develop my own arguments and theories. I was also given both responsibility and opportunity.

Now, don't get me wrong. I learned as a 20-something lawyer – just as I learned again when I was the 50-something employer of a 20-something lawyer – that the client wants the guy with the white hair. They want the experienced lawyer. They want who they paid for.

Other clients were happy to be charged the lower rates of the less experienced lawyer who was always overseen by the more experienced.

However, there was nothing more exhilarating than the time early in my tenure when my boss sent me to the Bronx ostensibly to adjourn a case with which I wasn't particularly familiar. Representing the wife, I was told that when the Judge asked what I wanted, I was to say, "We want him held in contempt." I was told by my boss that the Judge would tell me that a hearing was required and that the Court would adjourn the case to another day on which a hearing would be held.

That was what I was told.

Things do not always turn out as planned.

Me: *"Your Honor, the man is not paying, and we want him held in contempt!"*

Court: *"You know that requires a hearing, don't you?"*

Me: *"Of course, Your Honor."*

Court: *"Okay, call your first witness."*

What? That wasn't supposed to happen. But left with no other alternative, I called my client to the stand; I reviewed with her the Court-ordered obligations of her husband; and I elicited testimony proving that the husband was, in fact, in contempt having failed to meet those obligations.

What dry mouth? What nerves? Even though I had both, I knew that I had to just go forward. In the immortal words of Jack Webb (for those old enough to remember Dragnet!), *"Just the facts, ma'am!"*

This was not my first trial, but it was both the trial I was least prepared for and my shortest trial. But it was a winner. I felt good as did my client.

My first trial was also during the Ira years. I had a small hearing in the Family Court against an older female attorney who could not have been nicer to me. For the next few decades, until her own retirement, I would always remind her that she was *"my first"* and that she was *"gentle with me."* I always got a smile in return.

———

DURING MY TIME WITH IRA, I learned that the language of the settlement agreement is important.

We were representing a woman that I then thought of as "a little old lady." In truth, she was probably the same age then as I am now, some 40 years later.

Her ex-husband was suing her to have his alimony obligation terminated because she had been living with her boyfriend in La Jolla, California, in a resort community for several years.

Were this a divorce without an agreement and with the Judge having made the initial determination of alimony, as opposed to the agreement of the parties, the ex-husband would have had a valid argument to have his alimony eliminated based upon the cohabitation if that cohabitation were proven at trial. However, the parties had an agreement that provided for lifetime spousal support terminable *only* upon death or remarriage, with nothing else specified. Support would thus only end if one of the parties died or the wife had remarried. Such language was then commonplace as that was the language in the Internal Revenue Code at the time for the deductibility of alimony payments by the payor-spouse and includable as income to the recipient-spouse.

However, the agreement of these parties had no language about the termination of alimony upon the cohabitation of the wife, let alone defining language as to what constituted "cohabitation." (All of my agreements thereafter, when representing the alimony-paying spouse, contained specific language for termination of spousal support as well as having express terminology about how long the cohabitation needed to be to trigger the termination clause.)

Without the requisite language in the agreement of these parties, we were able to have the case summarily dismissed without the need for trial.

––––––

While with Ira, I experienced my first instance of multiple representations.

We had a client who had been Ira's client for a separate divorce before I started in his employ. I thought we were handling his second divorce. I later learned that he had been with our firm only for divorces three and four.

Some people are gluttons for punishment. I would think that if you had one or two divorces – divorces so acrimonious as to warrant representation by a high-conflict divorce specialist – you would learn that maybe marriage was not for them.

After I opened my own offices for the practice of law, I had another client who hired me for divorces from husbands #3 and #4 and then hired me again for a prenuptial agreement with husband #5. In fact, because the parties wanted to change their prenup after their marriage to provide my client with additional benefits, I also represented her in the negotiation and preparation of a post-nuptial agreement with #5.

––––––

Also while with Ira, there were many opportunities to use my creativity – and that I have always felt was one of my best attributes in practicing law.

We represented a woman who had an out-of-wedlock child with a noted entertainer. Were I to mention his name or his song titles, you would know him immediately. The client was one of the women who threw her panties on the stage at his concerts and who was then escorted backstage by his "people" to have a personal encounter with the star. The paternity trial that took place well before my involvement (I was still in law school at the time) was a pre-DNA paternity trial. Indeed, it was even before the Human Leucocyte Antigen (HLA) test that predated DNA testing. In other words, there was no science, let alone science recognized in law as evidence for the identification of the father. Rather, there was only ABO blood testing (types A, B, AB, and O) available for testing, and the law only permitted the use of such testing to exclude a man as a father – not to prove that a particular man was the father; that test or any other was not then allowable as proof of paternity, only for exclusion. Unlike a few years later when you could get a 99.9% chance of paternity through testing, science was not available to prove any man to be any child's father [and it still took the law a few more years after that to catch up with the science to allow for the admissibility of the DNA test in establishing paternity]. No, the standard of proof at that time was "opportunity, inclination, and intent," and those words mean what they say. There was a trial before I completed law school and thus was not involved at that time.

I became involved in the financial discovery stage, then the support trial, and the ultimate support appeal.

My argument was simple, although it was rejected by both the trial and appellate courts: Once a man is determined to be the father of the child, his support obligation should be the same as he would have regardless of whether the child was born in or out of wedlock. (I always detested the terms "legitimate" and "illegitimate;" the child is still the same regardless of the marital status of his/her parents, and there is no benefit to affixing this particular adjective.) As the entertainer had several other children born of his union with his wife, there was no reason to treat this newest child any differently from a financial point of view, particularly since neither mother earned any money at all. My argument was an esoteric equal protection theory under the United States Constitution, an argument that I believe should have been adopted then and an argument that is still viable now, some forty years later.

So, it was the night before our appellate brief was due; and I was in the middle of my first all-nighter since college. I was getting cabin fever and added a page to the Brief which quoted the entertainer's song titles evoking his efforts in seeking to avoid the consequences of love-making. I wrote that he was crying to the Court; and I literally used his most famous lyrics and song titles in my argument. I figured, what the heck, I had a boss who would surely edit this out. He did not.

My first foray into creative writing in a family law setting – not fiction, mind you, as I have described the writings of many, many other lawyers – proved good enough to pass the boss's review (or maybe he, himself, in the throes of an all-nighter, simply missed it). Unfortunately, the Appellate Division did not accept this argument. Nor did it even reference my clever plays on words in its published decision – perhaps because of the anonymous nature of the case name where the plaintiff was referenced by her first name and last initial, and the defendant was referenced by the same under his birth name (as opposed to his stage name).

Indeed, even my argument that the gentleman's tax returns showed that he tipped more than he was paying for the support of his child with my client fell upon deaf ears.

I can only surmise that the appellate court believed that sufficient child support was being paid.

———

ONE OF THE PROBLEMS with representing some women in paternity litigation against the uber-wealthy is that often; the mother considers the obligation owed to the child by the father as a means for their own support.

There is no palimony in New York, and the mother is not legally entitled to support for herself, only for the child.

Nevertheless, in far more than one instance – particularly when the case has been labeled by the Court with an "Anonymous" case title – the mother seeking support for her child has considered this her meal ticket. I have represented mothers in such matters both during my time as an employee attorney and after putting out my shingle for my own law practice.

I have represented several different women who felt that simply by giving birth to the child of a very rich man gave them some sort of personal entitlement above and beyond the support for the child. The law does not grant a mother of a child special rights of her own; it only provides that the child must be properly supported. This is a major distinction.

I have never been retained to represent the deep-pocketed alleged father in a paternity dispute. When representing the movie star who fathered the son of a television star, paternity was never in issue; and support had long since been resolved before I was retained during the ongoing custody and visitation issues. (Indeed, the mother's lawyer introduced himself to me by telling me, *"You know, you are his 19th lawyer?"* I told him, *"I might be his 19th lawyer, but I am the one you need to deal with!"* I have never reacted well to threats or intimidation. I often commented aloud, on the record and otherwise, that when the other side brought two, three, or even more lawyers to a proceeding to fight against *"li'l ole me."*)

I almost had my chance once to represent such an alleged father, but the ethical rules rightly prevented me from even meeting with the man. I got a call from a lifelong friend who was a commercial lawyer who regularly referred matters to me. He indicated that the son of his richest client – a man after whom buildings and hospitals were named – was the respondent in a paternity case. While I would normally have been ecstatic over the possibility of such a high-profile matter, I also knew that I had already met with a mother who claimed to have had her baby with a man having a similar background; that woman elected not to retain me. Further questioning from me revealed that the potential client my friend had for me was one and the same as the man alleged by the woman who previously sought my counsel. I was compelled to disclose the conflict of interest that prohibited me from evening consulting with the alleged father. I never even met with the man; I had no involvement whatsoever in the very lucrative litigation that ensued.

———

ON ANOTHER OCCASION, I was in Court in Brooklyn (at a time when this single Borough of the City of New York would have stood alone as the fourth most populated city in the United States) before the only Judge who had responsibility for every divorce in that County. I was making an argument; and the judge interrupted me: *"Mr. Bloom, is this one of Ira's shticks?"*

"No, Your Honor, it's one of my own."

Ira also provided me with as much autonomy as the various clients would allow.

Not only did I write most of the Briefs with little if any editing by the boss, but I argued motions and appeals (with the big paternity case and its related media attention being an exception), and also tried cases from start to finish.

The adversary did not matter. I went against new attorneys –

it was amazing how quickly I went from a rookie to one of the regulars to a seasoned pro to an old-timer. I went up against some of the biggest names in the field.

Indeed, on one occasion, I had my first example of Size Matters. I was in Court arguing a motion against a big attorney – big in both senses; he was well-known in the Courts and was physically huge. At six foot four, and at the time pushing 300 pounds, I was no lightweight; but this guy was taller than me and substantially outweighed me. The Judge called counsel to the Bench to have a private, off-the-record discussion with the lawyers about the case – which is where most of the decisions, if not settlements, are made. He and I approached the platform that was raised from the Court Room floor but still substantially below the Judge's Bench (seat), where he/she could still look down upon even the tallest lawyers. This other lawyer was making arguments while simultaneously using his elbow to literally push me aside. *"Excuse me, Your Honor,"* I interrupted; and then I turned to opposing counsel, and said, *"That type of intimidation might work with someone else, but it will not work with me. Stop it now!"* I don't think he had ever heard that before and backed away.

And the guy was not a stranger to me. He and other lawyers in his firm had worked with me on many cases through the years, both before and after this incident.

Karma is great. A few years later, a cover story in *The Sunday New York Times Magazine* featured this same formerly elbow-wielding lawyer and his Ponzi Scheme. He was soon after disbarred, never to be heard from again.

THAT EXPERIENCE PREPARED ME well for another incident years later at a time as I was practicing on my own when an even bigger name in the Matrimonial Bar (and only slightly less physically imposing than me) was negotiating with me in the Court hallway (another place where most of the work of litigating attorneys takes place). With our clients standing nearby, he asked me what I wanted to settle the case. I provided him with our plan for a resolution. His response was literally, *"Fuck you!"*

Even though I had heard these words before, I acknowledge having been somewhat taken aback by the language; it was a Court House after all, I put a smile on my face and my arm around his shoulder while telling him, *"You don't know me well enough to talk to me like that."*

We retreated to neutral corners.

An hour or so later (lots of time is wasted in Court), he made a counter-proposal to me. My response, I am sure you can guess, was a *"Fuck you,"* although mine was made with a big smile on my face.

About an hour after that, with the Judge pressuring lawyers on this and other cases to come to a resolution before the lunch break, we hashed out our clients' remaining differences and placed a settlement on the record.

———

ALSO, WHILE I HAD MY OWN PRACTICE, I had another case that was scheduled to be heard in an Upstate County.

As it turned out, this case was the only case on the docket of the particular Judge to whom our matter had been assigned.

Both parties and respective counsel appeared in the Judge's Courtroom at the appointed time. Indeed, because I had the furthest to travel, I had been in Court a good hour early.

The designated 9:30 a.m. time came and went. No Judge.

10 o'clock. No Judge.

The attorneys approached the Court Clerk without success, although the Clerk retreated to the back room.

Around 11:30, the Judge walked into the Courtroom wearing lime green pants and an equally hideous shirt, announcing [not on the record, of course], *"I have a tee time at 1 o'clock. You WILL settle this case before lunch!"*

We did.

It was amazing that the *"settle before lunch"* mandate achieved its desired effect.

CHAPTER 5
THE BREAK-UP

So that it is clear, I love the late Ira Richard Bennett, my mentor. Perhaps because he is no longer with us, I have no qualms about mentioning his name. But because of ethical considerations and because of his passing in 1990, his is the only name I will not change in this writing.

Ira gave me opportunity after opportunity. He respected me, and I him.

After all, I had never met, either before or after, a lawyer who when asked about an issue would give not merely the name of the case providing the authority for the determination of the resolution of the issue but more often than not would also give you the case citation (which amounted to a volume number, a reference to the Court level, and a page number).

But there are also two truths to being the second lawyer in a two-lawyer firm.

1. The client wants the guy with the white hair, the guy they paid for. This is true even when the young Turk has more energy, creativity, and sometimes even more devotion to the case than the white-haired boss.

2. Whatever money the second lawyer is earning is coming right out of the pocket of the first, thereby creating friction that destroys the bond over time. I would have thought – and I did think, both when an employee and later as an employer – that there was a way of pricing both what one paid the employee and what one charged the employee for the client's time that would make having a protegee/underling a profitable experience. I did not have that role model and was unable to find the happy median later in life as an employer.

This meant that Ira and I would have to part. Actually, we parted twice.

The first time was over money and money alone. I wanted more; and I could only get a higher salary with a competitor. I had received small raises over time, but not as much as I felt I deserved.

Looking around, I saw the big names and I saw the not-so-big names of the esteemed Matrimonial Bar of the City of New York.

Everyone knew Ira. Everyone respected his work. I had a foot in the door.

But the truth is that you need a really big ego to be successful in this field. Ira had it (before his passing in 1990). I had it and frankly still do. And, so did everyone with whom I interviewed for a new job.

I had an interview with one of the biggest names. I spoke with him for over an hour; and I knew the money that I would be paid by him would be very good. However, he was so pompous and full of himself that it became clear that, as I told him, *"Excuse me, I don't want to take any more of your time because I know that it is valuable, but I don't think we are a good fit."*

Decades later, well into my own new life after my personal divorce, I became friends with someone who had been represented by this guy. When I told her the story, she practically rolled on the floor with laughter as she knew him well and knew I had him pegged perfectly.

I found another job, this one in Suffolk County on Long Island. No big deal, I thought. Even though I was living on Manhattan's West Side, I was reverse commuting. The salary increase justified the travel time and expense.

But the truth was that I was both a fish out of water and had serious doubts about the trustworthiness of my boss. He certainly did not have the same stellar reputation that Ira had had.

As an example of the novelty of my physical surroundings, I did not know that the local town of Y-A-P-H-A-N-K was pronounced YAP-HANK. I had pronounced it YA-FANK, much to the amusement of my co-workers at this office. (Thankfully, I had not made this error in the Courtroom.)

I did not know the Suffolk County Judges; and I was given primary responsibility for the cases in Nassau and Queens Counties. We did not go any further west than Queens except for certain appellate work for these cases which were held in Brooklyn.

In this operation, the boss brought in the client and then immediately dealt the client out to one of the several associate attorneys in the firm. Occasionally, he would let his underlying attorneys do the initial client interview. There was considerable autonomy; and each of my clients came to realize very quickly that it was me, not the boss, who was entrusted with the day-to-day management of the litigation.

It also became apparent very quickly that my move, while certainly a financial step up, was not the right decision.

Even more quickly, Ira came to realize that I was pretty special myself. While he did not "woo" me, he certainly realized my worth, then matched and beat my new salary, and brought me back to Manhattan, as well as providing me with one of the best perks available – a parking spot in downtown Manhattan for which he paid.

This worked well for a while; and I did not have to push as hard for further modest raises.

However, I was once again the second choice of the clients.

I got antsy; and I was ultimately ready to make a change.

Then my Dad had a heart attack one day while we were on the golf course together. Triple bypass surgery followed. Of course, I took off to be with my family.

However, while Dad was still recuperating in the hospital, I knew that I would go stir-crazy sitting around all day. So, I called Ira and told him that I was going to come in but that I wanted to remain in the office and out of Court so that I would be reachable by phone in case of an emergency. (This was well before cell phones – even before the first generation of portable phones the size of a shoebox and the weight of a brick.)

"No problem," I was told and went to work. When I got to the office, he told me that we were going to Court in Brooklyn because there was a fee hearing and that I "might" be a witness. Even though I persisted in my request to be near a phone, I ultimately spent the entire day in Court, never once making an argument or taking the witness stand.

To say that I was a bit perturbed is an understatement. I was livid.

Leaving the Courtroom, I was in the elevator with Ira, the opposing counsel, and the Judge. (Now, Judges have their own elevators.)

I began an argument with Ira which ultimately ended as follows:

Ira: *You're fired!* [Maybe this was that other Apprentice.]

Me: *Don't bother! I quit!!!*

Not very mature, I know, but in retrospect it was the best thing that ever happened to me professionally.

CHAPTER 6
HIRING A DIVORCE LAWYER

THE FAMOUS ATTORNEY, Louis Nizer, in his seminal book, My Life in Court (1961), wrote with respect to the original War of the Roses (predating the movie of the same name) in which he represented one of the Roses, wrote:

> Litigations between husbands and wives exceed in bitterness and hatred those of any other relationships. I have represented defrauded businessmen who fight their deceivers for fortune and power. I have seen them pour out their venom against their opponents until they suffered heart attacks or were ulcerated. I have witnessed struggles for the protection of copyrighted property, where the pride of authorship, being dearer than life itself, consumed the creative artist. I have seen public figures libeled or accused of wrongs that could wreck their life's work, strike back at their detractors. I have observed men with spotless reputations who were indicted, suffer nervous breakdowns. I have witnessed children sue their fathers to deprive them of their businesses, or brothers engaged in fratricidal contests without quarter. I have seen defendants in antitrust suits beleaguered by

plaintiffs seeking treble damages or defending themselves against Government actions aimed to break up their enterprise, painstakingly built over a lifetime. I have participated in will contests in which relatives were at each others' throats for the inheritance.

All these litigations evoke intense feelings of animosity, revenge, and retribution. Some of them may be fought ruthlessly. But none of them, even in their most aggravated form, can equal the sheer, unadulterated venom of a matrimonial contest. The participants are often ready to gouge out the eyes or the soul of the once loved, without any pity whatsoever.

A man whose sense of honor may be punctilious and whose restraint under extreme provocation may be admirable, will unhesitatingly insist on making charges against his wife, which, even if true, would not be entertained by any decent man, particularly against the mother of his children. A woman who all her life has been kindly and gentle may turn so vengeful against her husband that she will write obscene and poisonous letters to his friends, create violent scenes at his office, confront and physically attack him in public places, have him arrested, and write anonymous accusations to the Treasury Department. Either may disregard their children's welfare by making them pawns in the battle, filling their ears with loathing for the other. There is no limit to the blazing hatred, the unquenchable vengefulness, the reckless abandonment of all standards of decent restraint, which a fierce matrimonial contest engenders.

I leave to the psychiatrists the explanation of the volatile transformation from love to hate. The chemical ingredients of rejection, jealousy, and possessiveness certainly play a part in the explosive content. But there is something more, a mysterious element, which unbalances the mind, changes the personality, and distorts the character. It derives undoubtedly from the sexual ties which, if profound and ecstatic, can never be completely severed. The mutual enslavement of love will not tolerate unilateral freedom. Two people joined together in intimacy are often like Siamese twins, the separation of one causing the death of the other. By great exercise of will, the rejected sometimes overcome the unbearable ache and readjust their lives. Even these go through an unsettling period that borders on the irrational. When one reads of a man of good repute and solid business judgment who has shot his wife and two children, or a woman of impeccable rearing and social status who has thrown acid into the eyes of her husband and then shot herself, the insanity of the rejected reaches its extreme manifestation. Short of such criminal violence, but stemming from the same acerbation of emotion, is the matrimonial lawsuit.

The lawyer is often caught in the fires that rage about him. The other half of the erstwhile union cannot, of course, believe that the gentle person of prior intimate experience has turned out to be so characterless. The conclusion is easy: "It's the lawyer who is putting him up to it. Bill could never do anything so rotten," or "It's the lawyer's scheme. Mary just isn't that kind of a woman." Since the lawyer should serve as a lightning rod, to draw the bolts away from his client, he must consider the injustice done to him a necessary professional sacrifice.

Who am I to dispute the eloquent Mr. Nizer?

My experience tells me that sometimes it is the client, and sometimes it is the lawyer who is to blame for the venom in divorce litigation. An angry litigant comes to a lawyer's office seeking to move on in his or her life. We take our clients as we find them. Or, we don't take them at all. Often, the rejection of the case and the election not to take on a particular client's matter is the most appropriate decision a lawyer can make. Even when facing economic realities, the best alternative is to stay away from some cases. Of course, I have also been guilty of accepting a retainer fee from a client I should have declined for the simple reason that quarterly taxes were due the following week.

The divorce lawyer is not a psychotherapist and most definitely cannot "change" a client.

And sometimes, it is the lawyer who throws lighter fluid on the embers to inflame the client on the embers that could have easily been quelled. I have certainly had adversaries that fall into that category.

The client, often emotional and distraught, must not be misled.

So, the question is: How does one select a divorce lawyer?

I have always used an analogy, admittedly more appropriate for women than for men. (In fact, far more often, it is the female who seeks advice on the selection of counsel, while men do not make such a request of divorce lawyers, instead relying on referrals from their business attorneys.)

"Think of it as buying a pair of shoes. Interview prospective lawyers; in essence, try on a few pairs. When you are comfortable (and confident) with the lawyer and his or her approach, that is the one for you."

If you are uncomfortable with anything at all in that initial meeting, find another lawyer. There are plenty of divorce lawyers. You can ask someone you know who got divorced about who to hire; that person is usually happy to tell you to use his/her lawyer, or not use that lawyer – or to use or not use their spouse's lawyer. I have always loved getting a referral of a prospective client because I represented someone's spouse and had done a good job. Everyone knows of a lawyer; you can ask that lawyer for a referral of someone who concentrates on matrimonial law.

But what do you ask? How do you try them on?

First and foremost, is the lawyer a generalist or a specialist? Does the lawyer have a general practice where he or she only dabbles in divorce work; or does the lawyer concentrate on family-related matters? I would advise against the general practitioner as he or she may not be as well versed in the intricacies of matrimonial practice as would a lawyer who devotes virtually all of his/her efforts to divorce matters.

After that, the most important thing is to learn about the approach that the lawyer takes to matrimonial litigation and to your own needs.

All divorce lawyers want to get the best possible result for their clients. In the law, like in life, no one likes to lose. More so than in the general population, lawyers have big egos that simply will not allow them to lose.

However, different lawyers have different opinions about what is the best possible result.

Furthermore, for every divorce lawyer, there is a unique plan on how to achieve that best possible result. Indeed, many attorneys have several alternative strategies for obtaining the best result depending upon the needs of the particular client and their various priorities.

In some instances, that means negotiating to resolve all issues in dispute.

Indeed, there is an entire subspecialty of divorce law called collaborative law. In collaborative law, at the outset, the two clients do not merely sign a retainer agreement with their respective lawyers, but the two clients and their two lawyers also all sign a collaboration agreement which includes a provision that they will not commence litigation and with the understanding that if a party does start a lawsuit against the other, the two lawyers will be disqualified from representation of their client in the litigation. Some matrimonial lawyers only practice in a collaborative setting.

Collaborative law is an effective mechanism when both parties are committed to negotiation. Collaboration creates an environment where even positions in polar opposites can find a middle ground.

However, there are many instances when collaboration simply will not work. Often, a spouse who has always gotten his way (or her way) during the course of the marriage may believe that he or she can deal with the divorce in the same way, believing that his/her way has worked before and it will work again. Other times there is the spouse that sabotages the negotiations by unreasonably refusing to compromise. Sometimes, at least one of the spouses has a "drop dead" position on which he or she simply will not budge.

More often than not, the factual circumstances demand that the intervention of a Court is necessary. Those instances include domestic violence, a threatened removal of a child from the jurisdiction, or where one spouse has closed a bank account or threatens to do so. Such a unilateral act by a spouse demands that the other bring on a formal lawsuit and seek interim relief from the Court. Such is not a setting where collaborative law will be appropriate.

The other extreme is the divorce lawyer who says, "*I like to try cases.*" Those attorneys believe that every divorce starts with the commencement of a formal divorce action in Court as opposed to starting with a letter to the other spouse asking that he or she retain counsel to try to work out a negotiated agreement. Ira "liked to try cases," as have many other attorneys that I have encountered in four decades of practice.

Whenever I hear from another lawyer, "I like to try cases," it is a giant red flag. It tells me that the lawyer cares more about him/herself than about the client.

It is the client and the circumstances of the case that must dictate how the litigation is to commence and then proceed. Dire or emergent situations demand immediate action that requires the lawyer to go to Court without delay. Where the issues are straightforward, and the facts are not in dispute, particularly when no children are involved, a simple letter that serves as an invitation to negotiation is best. If your client is terrified of a courtroom, the commencement of judicial proceedings is usually not advised and only used as an alternative in dire circumstances.

In short, it is not about what the lawyer wants or about the lawyer's ego. It is about what the particular client needs.

My personal preference is that unless it is necessary, the invitation-to-negotiation letter is the best first approach. There is no reason to file and serve papers – to throw down the proverbial gauntlet – when circumstances do not demand immediacy.

The letter is simple:

> *Dear Mr./Mrs. So-and-so,*
> *Your spouse has consulted with me as to your marital diffi-*
> *culties.*
> *We are desirous of an amicable agreement.*
> *Please have your attorney contact me at the earliest opportunity.*
> *Very truly yours,*
> *LHB*

The results of this invitation will be limited.

One would hope that within a week or two after the letter is sent, the spouse will have retained counsel that will have reached out to me to begin negotiations.

Another extreme is that the spouse will retain counsel that aggressively commences a divorce action without so much as a phone call to me – not even to ask if I would accept service of process on behalf of my client. While this is not enviable, it is not unusual. An experienced matrimonial attorney is fully equipped to deal with this and to mark in his/her memory bank the type of lawyer the adversary will be as the litigation proceeds.

The most common response to the invitation-to-negotiation

letter is a nonresponse. The spouse simply ignores the lawyer's letter. In those instances – and again, when there is no reason for emergency action – a slightly stronger letter will be used two or three weeks after the first letter:

> *Dear Mr./Mrs. So-and-so,*
>
> *My records indicate that on [date], I sent you a letter, a copy of which is enclosed.*
>
> *While we are still amenable to an amicable resolution of the issues, we need to hear from your lawyer as soon as possible.*
>
> *Failure to respond within two weeks of the date hereof will necessitate the commencement of formal litigation.*
>
> *I hope to hear from your attorney before that time.*
>
> *Very truly yours,*
>
> *LHB*

After that, the lawyer must make good on his/her ultimatum and start the divorce action; a failure to act would send a message indicating weakness.

If you have particular concerns about what might happen or you have certain must-haves in the divorce case, tell the lawyer those things in the initial consultation with that lawyer. From the very start, it will allow the lawyer to focus on your most important concerns.

CHAPTER 7
MY PRACTICE

So, after my final breakup with Ira, there I was, barely 30 years old with a new wife. And no job. Thank God we were not yet expecting our first child.

Needless to say, I was scared out of my wits.

But word traveled fast.

One friend of Ira's friends learned of this development with Ira's office (that is, me) and called me at home the very next day, making me an offer that worked out great for both of us.

I was offered my own office with no rent; and I was also to be provided with the use of both the telephone and the support staff.

His idea was that he would stop sending his contested divorces to Ira and keep these cases for himself with me doing the work. We would equally divide the legal fees. I was also free to develop my own practice.

The first six months of this arrangement put more money in my pocket than what I had earned in the prior twelve months with Ira.

Plus, I was never second-guessed. I was the primary attorney for the clients from the very beginning. No client thereafter ever asked for the "other guy" to go to Court with them, argue their motions, or try their cases.

At roughly the same time, my old roommate, a real estate attorney in Queens practicing with his father and another lawyer, needed my assistance. The attorney in their firm, who was not his father, a matrimonial attorney himself, was undergoing triple bypass surgery (at a time when it was still major surgery needing a long recuperation time). They needed someone to step into the litigation practice and offered me a partnership.

In retrospect, the prudent move would have been to accept this position. However, with the new arrangement with Ira's "friend," I was earning more than ever; and I did not like the idea of having to answer to a partner. As with the Law Review article, I worked best on a schedule of my own choosing. I did not (and still to this day do not) work well and play well with others for many reasons, including that *my way is the right way."*

Nevertheless, my friend and his Dad needed help; and I was not averse to additional income. I suggested a trial partnership where I came to the Queens office two days per week where I worked on my cases as well as their cases, while also working in the Manhattan office the other days again still working on my cases and their cases.

One noteworthy thing about the work in the Queens office was that the clients were skewed female and were much better looking than my other clientele. Indeed, the most beautiful client that I ever had was from this office. More on that later.

Eventually, my friend's partner fully recovered and returned to the office. This provided me with the justification to return full-time to Manhattan.

I would later become a practicing New Jersey attorney, first using my home as my New Jersey office before renting space from a colleague in Bergen County near my own marital residence. I also later developed a large Westchester County when I essentially became the in-house counsel of a parents' rights group in that County; and I rented another office in that County for a few years for the convenience of burgeoning Westchester practice. Maintaining three offices was burdensome, but I was working many hours each week and making good money. I was able to carry the financial obligations.

But early in my own practice, I was young and hungry, and maybe a little naïve. I started taking whatever I could get in terms of legal work. While I knew I was a matrimonial attorney in my heart, my wallet screamed to be filled. No potential client was turned away. (Only years later did I learn the wisdom in just saying, "*No, thank you.*")

This also caused me to expand my practice geographically by adding Federal Court admissions to three of the four District Courts in New York (not the Western District), the District Court of New Jersey, the Circuit Court of Appeals for the Third Circuit covering New Jersey and Pennsylvania (but not the Second Circuit which included New York), and the United States Supreme Court. Being admitted to these Courts did not mean that I actually practiced there; it just meant that I was legally allowed to practice in those courts. I sought admission to the Third Circuit because I had stupidly taken on a non-matrimonial commercial collection case in the District of New Jersey that I wanted to be able to handle in the event that there was an appeal. I obtained admission to the United States Supreme Court because of a Hague Convention case that I was then trying. The Hague Convention is an international treaty governing child custody disputes extending beyond our country's borders; and the U.S. Supreme Court has ultimate jurisdiction in the interpretation of international treaties. As this was probably the most interesting case I ever tried (not to mention the most lucrative), I needed to make sure that I was admitted to The Supreme Court as a prophylactic insurance policy in the event that this divorce involving the issue of whether the divorce the children would be allowed to live in New York or be required to be returned to Switzerland.

I never even saw the Third Circuit Courthouse in Philadelphia; and I was only in the United States Supreme Court building on a childhood trip with my parents to Washington, D.C.

At around the time that I was taking on virtually any case that walked through my door, I developed what I called my "pro bono criminal practice." I never wanted to do criminal work; and I steered away from those cases after my first job in general practice. However, I had a family; and I had friends with family. Those people, usually their 20-something progeny, had gotten into trouble; and those were the criminal cases I could neither turn down nor charge a fee. Hence, its *pro bono* nature.

Some interesting stories developed from these, particularly while representing my wife.

I was once in my hometown in New Jersey, a small town with but a single traffic light, representing my wife, who had a traffic infraction. While I knew the prosecuting attorney from town, I had never seen the judge before. Here is how the appearance went:

Judge: *Mr. Prosecutor, you want Mr. Bloom to be able to go home tonight, don't you?*

Prosecutor: *Yes, Your Honor.*

Judge: *Case dismissed.*

That was it.

On another occasion, she was caught allegedly speeding on the Palisades Interstate Parkway. So much of the maintenance of this roadway was funded by the ticketing of motorists, that it had its own Court where they charged exorbitant fines.

The Court House was packed, mostly with people charged with speeding, some parents and their children, or other people representing themselves, with very few lawyers in the room. However, I knew the drill: get there early, speak with the prosecutor in another room, cut a deal for a fine with no insurance points, get your case called early, and get the hell out of there.

While awaiting the availability of the prosecutor (he had to be present before the Judge to hear the first criminal non-traffic cases), the non-traffic cases were heard. There were about ten cases where the defendant was a male senior citizen charged with "indecent exposure." My wife whispered to me about what she considered *"a surprising number of perverts,"* to which I replied, *"They're not perverts; they had to pee!"*

This is the kind of Court it was. To top that off, the Judge showed no leniency towards these elderly gentlemen. No, they were not going to jail, but they were being fined an incredible amount for doing nothing worse than answering the call of nature.

By the time the prosecutor and I agreed on what the resolution would be (a fine with minimal insurance "points"), the Judge had just finished the first call of a very long calendar. He had left the Bench, but the room still had the Courtroom Quiet atmosphere. I walked in where my wife was sitting in the front row; and I said to her in not a hushed tone, *"I got you a great deal. You only have to spend one night in jail!"*

The collective gasp from the back of the room was deafening.

Maybe this is part of the reason that she is now my ex-wife.

The kids of friends and family presented other issues.

For years and years, I had a barter system with my friend, who was also married to my wife's first cousin – making him still my friend but now my ex-cousin. I would do the family's legal work in exchange for him doing my family's dental work. (Frankly, I think I got the better of this deal.) I represented him, his wife, and two of his three kids. The one I did not represent was the one I wanted to handle, but the son wanted a different cousin-attorney. Why did I want the case? The charge was "driving while naked." How much fun would that have been?!?

However, in these settings, you do get a further appreciation (or lack thereof) of family. Friends are friends out of choice; but let's face it, you don't get to pick your family – not even your in-laws.

Another cousin, while attending college in Upstate New York, had an anger issue when his girlfriend decided she needed a change in their relationship status. My cousin's reaction was to throw a garbage drum through the large plate glass window of his dormitory. His first visit to Court was met with a furious judge who gave him a date to come back with the admonition, *"Next time, bring a parent and a lawyer!!!"*

For Court appearance number 2, I flew Upstate for the day with the "client's" father (who was and is also one of my best friends). As is typical in cases like these as well as traffic offenses, the first step is a meeting outside the Courtroom alone with the prosecutor. I left my client and his dad alone to meet with the prosecutor, his assistant, and a summer intern in the prosecutor's office. After talking about other things (in this case, the new danger of being an intern just after a Congressional intern had gone missing) to develop some kind of rapport with the other side on a case on which I had no defense, we get to the matter at hand. *"Mr. Bloom, we know you traveled all the way up from New York City; but is it okay if we give your client a conditional dismissal of the charges pending 50 hours of community service?"*

"Hell no!" I responded, *"Give him more! I want to make sure he learns his lesson!"*

Before the Judge rubberstamped the deal, I went back to the clients to see if the 75 hours of community service that I had "negotiated" was acceptable. It was; and the young man thanked me profusely. *"You really want to thank me?"* I answered, *"Don't make me do this again!"*

I told his father the extent of the negotiations as the two of us flew back that evening; and he loved it. As for the client himself, his reading of this will be his first knowledge of what transpired. Hopefully, he will not be too upset about having to coach Little League for a few extra hours.

Every time I needed to represent a teenager/20-something, the parent always came for emotional (and often, financial) support. Indeed, when one of my children had a traffic issue, I went not as counsel (the mother of that child's then significant other, a local attorney in that town's court, appeared as counsel) but as the concerned parent.

Every time, except once. A young man, whose bris I had attended decades before as one of my first adventures with my new Orthodox Jewish family of extended in-laws, was faced with a serious legal issue arising out of a traffic matter where he was driving what he thought to be his friend's car – it wasn't. Of course, I would take the day to make sure he received proper legal protections. But much to my amazement, neither parent came with him as I had never been on such a criminal case without one parent being there for his/her child's support. Faced with a very real possibility of jail time or certainly something more substantial than a stain on his permanent record, neither parent saw fit to travel with their child to the Courthouse.

To say the least, my opinions of and dealings with those first cousins of my wife were permanently impacted. I simply lost all respect for them. Of course, with my divorce, these became my ex-relatives with whom I have had no contact but for weddings in my family.

But, again, I digress.

My job remained as a divorce attorney.

———

Certainly, there was no shortage of people who were in marriages that were felt to need termination.

As I have said, my practice with Ira and then for decades thereafter in my own firm focused on the hotly contested divorces where the parties truly hated one another.

While there was some internet advertising as well as referrals through networking, the great bulk of my cases were referrals from other lawyers. When they had an "easy divorce," they usually kept it for themselves – or at least until they messed the case up before sending the client to me to clean up after them. But the ones that had the potential for being contested were farmed out to me, particularly where the last divorce the referring lawyer had had was against me on the other side.

I guess that was a compliment, although even better was when the cases were referred by one of my former client's former spouse. *"Hire my wife's lawyer! He really put me over the coals!"* Clients like that were presold on me before they ever walked into my office.

CHAPTER 8
EVOLUTION

AFTER A FEW YEARS, I realized that taking on every type of legal case was a bad decision. I began to weed out everything but the family law-related cases.

As time went on, the expansion of my practice led to a contraction. Federal Court cases quickly became a thing of the past (although I remained ready, willing, and able to travel to D.C. to argue my Hague Convention case before The Supreme Court should that have been warranted). When I was later asked about whether I took cases in Federal Court, I always responded by saying, *"I don't like to go to Federal Court. They make you act like a lawyer there!"*

The Federal Court collections case cured me not only of the Federal Court but of collections cases in general.

Real estate law had been a side venture representing family and friends who were buying or selling a home. But that truly was as boring as it had been years before when working my first job as a lawyer. Real estate quickly was eliminated, particularly after my secretary threatened to quit if we handled more of them

– and we were doing her mother's purchase of her new home *pro bono* at the time.

Even the divorce and family cases that I handled contracted, albeit the contraction was in geographic area. I had represented a father in a child neglect proceeding in Sussex County, New Jersey (almost a two-hour drive from my Northeastern New Jersey home) involving his six children. Court appearances for neglect cases in that County were always on Tuesday afternoons at 1:30 p.m. just after the Court's lunch break; and I was required to be there promptly at 1:30 even though the Judge routinely kept my case with several different lawyers (representing the State that prosecuted these types of cases, counsel for each parent and many lawyers for the various children because of the special needs that each had) for last on the docket for the day. This Judge also did not believe in a definitive closing time (in most Courts judges leave the bench by 4:00 p.m. with only an occasional extension but never past 4:30 for the simple reason that the union for the Court Officers – the guys with the guns – was so strong that there was usually no convincing them to stay late). Indeed, on more than one occasion, this particular neglect case was not even called until well past 5:00 p.m.; and with each lawyer needing to be heard, argument by everyone encompassed well over an hour. I often did not get home until after 8:00 p.m.

Although that matter presented very interesting legal issues, as did another case I had in Monticello, New York (also two hours from my home) for which I was retained by the pre-teen children in a custody dispute between their parents, I realized that the amount of driving just was not worth either the effort or the fee. (They had heard of me in the media after representing the movie star dad against the television star mom.)

As an aside to the Sussex County neglect case, two decades after my involvement concluded, I received a call from the youngest child of that family wanting me to represent her in her own divorce. Talk about feeling old!

Over time, I eliminated those types of cases in my field that were geographically undesirable but also those for which I had true distaste.

In fact, there were some cases that were within my bailiwick and professional wheelhouse -- and at which I was well experienced and truly good at – that I eliminated over the decades.

Those cases involved allegations of child sexual abuse. Later on, I started to decline representation in all types of child abuse matters.

But, first as an employee and later as a young solo practitioner, I couldn't or at least wouldn't simply say, *"No thank you,"* the most important three words that a lawyer learns during his professional career. The biggest regrets had always been the cases that I had taken on as opposed to those upon which I had passed.

In my stint working in Suffolk County, I alone interviewed a prospective client who came in to obtain representation for an appeal of a finding that he had sexually abused his very young child. I had the most appellate experience of the five lawyers in the office, including the boss. Why my boss was not present for this initial interview is now lost to my memory. This man (and he was no gentleman) brought with him the 25-page findings of the Trial Judge that were graphic and left nothing to the imagination. In fact, the crimes that he had been found to have committed against his very, very young child disgusted me – and it has historically taken a very long time for me to feel that way about anything. (I never judged my clients, but in this instance, how could I not take these trial findings into my decision about whether to take on the appeal?)

Before we discussed any appealable grounds (that would be the rulings and other things that might have served as the basis of an appeal), I asked him about the contents of the trial decision.

The prospective client never denied the allegations made against him, never gave any excuse for his conduct (not that there could have been any), and never showed any inkling of remorse. Knowing that if this guy retained our office, I would be the primary attorney representing this man – not only because I was assigned the initial interview but also because I had the most appellate practice experience of all the attorneys in the firm – I did not want to represent him. No how, no way. But what to do?

Well, my boss would have been very happy had we received a $10,000 retainer fee for the appeal. Despite this, I asked for $25,000. Son of a gun, the guy almost paid it, much to my amazement. He said he only had $15,000 and wanted a payout of the balance. I told him we were sorry, but our policy was not to accept payouts of retainer fees. "*I want to be your lawyer, not your banker.*" Those became words oft-repeated over the next 35 years, even though, at least in this first instance, I had no desire whatsoever to represent this man for any amount of money.

Another case involving alleged sexual abuse of a child was also memorable, lasting several years over many different litigations.

I represented a firefighter who was a large man. As I previously noted, I bear a relatively imposing figure, well over six feet tall and then being unreasonably close to 300 pounds. But this guy towered over me; and while he approached my weight, he was pure muscle as opposed to the flab that I carried. He also had extremely large hands.

His wife had alleged that he had sexually abused his four-year-old son. What had actually happened was that while he was helping the boy wipe after defecating, my client pushed too hard and drew a little blood.

One would think this was a simple case that should have been disposed of quickly. But the mother would not let go of the idea that her little boy had been "abused."

This case was in Brooklyn's Family Court. One of the differences between the Supreme and Family Courts is that trials almost never continue on consecutive days in the Family Court. The Family Court is overwhelmed with all types of family cases; and calendars there are tightly packed, sometimes having 20 cases or more on each judge's calendar for the day. Before the Supreme Court, it is possible to get four days of trial in a week (with one day being set aside for the Court's motion day when it hears motions on as many as 20 different cases in a single day); and sometimes you can get a trial to continue over two consecutive weeks. On one occasion, I had a five-week trial where we were given almost all day every day of the week (with only a few hours on a single day per week set aside for motions in other matters). However, each Family Court Judge has a large calendar with many cases every single day. A trial before the Family Court is usually limited to the after-the-lunch break session (usually only an hour or two of it); and whenever the Judge wanted to stop for the day, you were told to come back on a date two months later.

This particular large-hand wiping small-tushie case had no less than fifteen different days of testimony but those trial days extended over two years.

Thankfully, we prevailed.

But that was not the end of it. The mother would not let it go. She insisted over the years that my client "abused" "*her*" (not "*their*") son on the prior occasion as well as at other times she manufactured. The case was assigned to the same Judge who eventually lost patience with the mother and indicated that if she did not stop these false allegations, which in and of themselves were considered to be child abuse by her, she was risking losing custody of the child.

The mother persisted. I brought on a change of custody proceeding in the Supreme Court divorce action that was assigned to the very same Judge who had previously heard the prior abuse allegations, who by then had been promoted from the Family Court to Supreme.

After yet another trial, Dad wound up with full legal custody of his son.

I should note that even wins like this for which I was extremely happy, albeit taking several years, could not make these cases any more palatable for me.

Many years later when a woman facing charges of child abuse came to me for a defense, I questioned her about the allegations against her. I asked if there was any merit to the claims of abuse, specifically asking if she hit her child. Her response was, *"He's my kid. I can hit him if I want."*

I declined representation of this particular matter without too much further discussion between us, never reaching the matter of legal fees. I simply did not want to represent such a client.

CHAPTER 9
FUN LAW

Divorce law is generally not fun. People are experiencing some of the worst moments of their lives, and there is nothing fun about that.

Nevertheless, there were two areas of family practice that are, in fact, fun.

———

Unquestionably, the best part of being a family law attorney is doing adoption work.

Whether it is a family adoption, a foster parent adoption, or a private adoption, the process joins a parentless child with a new family, sometimes providing that child with siblings with the occasional blood sibling thrown in the mix when adopting parents choose a child from the same biological parents. It provides childless couples with the child they have always dreamed of having, or an otherwise unexpected sibling for the child or children they already have.

However, adoption law is basically ministerial in nature. It's just paperwork, with the only Court appearance being what Ira used to call "Lollypop Day." The lawyer and adopting parents would go before the Judge, usually with their new baby on their laps or small child sitting next to them, to go through a pro forma script for the finalization of the adoption.

After a few questions from the Judge, he or she would proclaim the adoption complete, and then hand the adoptive child a lollypop.

Everyone was happy – surprisingly, the Judge was the happiest, as the adoption day was a respite from the abuse and neglect cases, the domestic violence cases, and the vitriolic custody cases that ordinarily filled the Family Court docket.

Adoptions are fun for the lawyer for the exact same reason.

Although the paperwork regularly stalled as Court staff viewed adoption as non-emergent, often assigning the Adoption Clerk to other more immediate activities.

But the payoff of seeing broad smiles on everyone's faces was always well worth it.

———

THE ONLY DOWNSIDE of the adoption practice was the prospective parents looking to buy a baby and the mothers looking to sell one.

Quite often, I was presented with this situation from a prospective client fitting one of these categories.

Part of the bureaucratic paperwork sought sworn statements from everyone involved about the compensation paid and received by the parties, including the compensation received by the lawyer. The payment of childbirth expenses by the adopting parents was allowable, as were the payment of reasonable legal fees. But, the process was designed to make sure that baby selling was not taking place. It put the fear of suspension and disbarment in the attorney.

I viewed baby brokering – that was often what I was being sought to perform – as reprehensible; and I always saw the loss of my license as the ultimate result of involvement in these cases.

Legitimate adoption law was one thing. Baby brokering was completely another.

I remained vigilant in the avoidance of such a career-ending representation – not to mention a conscience-destroying endeavor.

———

THE OTHER AREA OF FUN is the prenuptial agreement, commonly known as the prenup.

Perhaps only a divorce lawyer would find this one of the more memorable lines in movie history. At the very beginning of the movie *Private Benjamin*, there is a scene in the hotel room on the wedding night of the title character, played by Goldie Hawn, to a divorce lawyer, played by Albert Brooks. Albert is on the phone, and with glee in his voice, he says, *"Prenups, baby!"* (in the same tone as Vince Vaughn would years later say, *"Vegas, baby!"* in Swingers).

A prenuptial agreement is a situation involving two people in love. At least one of the parties wants to protect either his or her assets, and/or his or her children of a prior relationship.

Usually, the parties don't enter into a prenup and then plan a wedding. It is almost always the other way around, with a wedding date set, and only then does one of the betrothed raise the issue of a prenup.

Thus, when the lawyers are first retained, there is an end date to the representation.

The goal is to complete the legal work within a very short period to allow the parties to meet the wedding date deadline.

The lawyers also need to complete their work and have the agreement properly executed (meaning, with certain formalities, including the people signing before a notary) sufficiently before the wedding so that there cannot be a subsequent challenge to the agreement as being executed under duress. The usual rule of thumb is that a prenup signed the day before, or even the day of, the wedding is buying a future lawsuit to set aside the prenup on this ground if the parties do not live happily ever after. It does not mean that the prenuptial agreement is doomed to failure and may be set aside, but the parties could very well run that risk; and this risk of litigation about the validity of the prenup defeats the innate purpose of the prenup itself.

Similarly, it is always a good idea to have an independent lawyer represent each party to the prenup to avoid potential challenges to it on the grounds of duress, overreaching, or even unconscionability. Again, why avoid the possibility of future litigation, the uncertainty, and the chance of the agreement being declared null and void if, by having a lawyer on each side, you could avoid it?

The fact that the people are in love and want to marry quickly should take the prenup out of the divorce lawyers' ordinary posturing.

Unfortunately, there are many matrimonial attorneys writing prenuptial agreements that cannot adjust their mindset away from the adversarial battleground.

I always had a motto when handling a prenup: stating to the other side, "*Let's not divorce these people before they even get married. It is a happy time for them. We want to protect our clients without driving an irreparable wedge between them.*"

As an example, as one of my first matters after leaving Ira's employ, I became involved in the negotiations of a prenup with only a week to go before the wedding celebration.

I received a referral from a friend of a friend of a first-time bride. Her family literally came over to America on the *Mayflower*; to say she was "old money" does a disservice to the word "old." She had been represented by one of the large white-shoe law firms in Manhattan.

The groom was going on marriage #2, with older children from his first marriage. He owned a substantial number of apartment buildings on the Upper West Side. He was "new money" and had already experienced a bad divorce. He was represented by another large firm with a renowned matrimonial department.

The problem was that the lawyers were treating the matter as a divorce and fighting about everything as they tried to hammer out a deal; and the hammer they were using was a sledgehammer. Indeed, when my client fired her fancy lawyers and came to me, she brought a draft of a 30+ page document (exclusive of the extensive addendum listing their specific assets).

She wanted it to be simplified and done so fast. The wedding was only days away. She loved the man but hated all the lawyers.

With my assistance, we carved the agreement down to absolute necessities, bringing it into a still-verbose ten pages (although the addendum defining which asset of the many assets belonged to each spouse necessarily remained – but the addendum was not lawyer-created).

During these final negotiations, I took the position that these parties were getting married, not getting divorced. With my assistance, the agreement was signed early in the week of the wedding. Most importantly, the parties remained in love with each other as they walked down the aisle.

As NOTED, it is better to have a lawyer representing each of the spouses-to-be on the prenup.

Often, the party with less valuable assets either does not want a lawyer or cannot afford one.

During those situations, it is not uncommon for the lawyer of the wealthier fiancé(e) to recommend a lawyer to the other; nor is it uncommon for the wealthier fiancé(e) to foot the legal expense for that other attorney.

A good rule of thumb is for the agreement to specify when one party is paying the other's legal fees to avoid a subsequent challenge that the lesser-monied party had been snookered into signing an agreement not knowing that his/her lawyer was in the pocket of the other.

A lawyer recommending another to the other side is not doing so to take advantage of (or snooker) the other party, even though the recommended lawyer could be considered to be a friend. Rather, it is done to cut through the attorney posturing that often takes place when lawyers first meet. It is akin to the *"mine's bigger"* argument one might hear in a locker room or a play-ground. This allows the lawyers to cut to the chase to discuss whatever may be truly objectionable in the prenup that is under consideration a short time before a scheduled wedding.

I have been brought into cases by "friends," or at least lawyers with whom I have previously had a good relationship. At other times, I have brought in lawyers to represent the other side.

One day, a lawyer whom I had known for years, a lawyer 30 years my senior, brought me in to represent the bride-to-be a couple of weeks before the upcoming nuptials. A lawyer was needed to represent the fashion model who was marrying her dermatologist, my friend's client.

After my first meeting with the client, I called this father figure of an attorney, and I told him, *"I'm sorry. My client cannot marry your client."*

"Why not?"

"Because I want to marry her!"

After a laugh, we got on to business, negotiated a prenup fair for both sides and allowed the two to live happily ever after.

———

WHENEVER I LEARN OF PEOPLE – friends, relatives, acquaintances, really anyone – who was getting married, I always recommend a prenup.

"Why? We don't have anything."

Or, *"Why? Neither of us have kids."*

"It doesn't matter," I tell them.

Then, I "sell" them on the idea of a prenup. (I never "sell" a divorce. Either the parties want a divorce, or they don't. There is no need to "sell" them on the divorce itself. In those instances, I only "sell" myself.)

"Listen," I tell them. *"Your marriage is going to end; and it is going to end in one of only three ways. There is no other option. Either you are going to die, or your spouse is going to die, or you are going to get divorced."*

"Since you know of these three scenarios for the end of your marriage, doesn't it make sense to deal with each of these three eventualities? That is what the prenup does."

One of the main reasons people have prenuptial agreements, particularly where at least one of the parties has children of a prior relationship, is to opt out of the marital election. Without the opt-out language where the parties waive their claims in the estates of the other, the statutory law (New York's Estates, Powers and Trusts Law, also called the EPTL) provides the surviving spouse with rights to claim against the estate of their deceased spouse. If a married person dies without a will or dies with a will that does not provide the surviving spouse with a sufficient amount (sometimes nothing at all), the surviving spouse may make a "marital election" against the estate. Only the waiver language of the marital estate that is usually contained in a prenuptial agreement will allow a spouse to disinherit the surviving spouse – as the children of the deceased's prior relationships give a sigh of relief.

———

A PRENUPTIAL AGREEMENT can include anything. But some topics should be included and other things that should be excluded.

Division of specific assets upon the demise of the marriage by death or divorce – usually the assets that each party brought into the marriage – should be addressed in the prenup. You can also address assets that the parties may acquire during the marriage. The parties can even agree, if they wish, that title will be controlling in the event of a divorce even though the parties may live in an equitable distribution or community property State. In those cases, the contractual understanding of the parties will supersede the otherwise applicable statutory mechanism for the division of property.

The parties may mutually agree to waive any future claim to spousal support from the other, or they can agree to their own formula for spousal support upon divorce. Again, this would supersede the normal mechanism for determining maintenance for a party. There are only a few limitations on this, as the Courts will not allow a party to become a "public charge." They will not allow tax dollars to be spent to support a needy party when that party's spouse can provide support.

However, the parties may not agree to a child custody arrangement or a visitation plan for the children they may have in the future. The Courts, that is, the State, serve as *parens patraie,* to the child. The Courts are obligated to ensure that the best interests of the child are met. There are also child support guidelines applicable to the ongoing support of the offspring of parties to a divorce based upon the time-of-divorce earnings of the respective parents. The rights of the children not yet in existence cannot be properly waived by either parent in a prenup or other type of agreement.

Then, some things should not be in a prenup.

I have often been asked about a prenuptial agreement that will be self-terminating. Usually, they are asking for an agreement that will extinguish itself after a certain period of time such as the parties' tenth wedding anniversary.

There is a commonly told story around the Matrimonial Bar of a pair of movie stars who married with such a prenup set to dissolve on the parties' tenth wedding anniversary. At the time of the marriage, he was far more successful than she. Nine and a half years later, he was still more successful than she, although the gap between them had narrowed substantially. Today, after her Academy Award and other accolades, they are equally famous and among the most successful actors in the business.

Shortly before their tenth anniversary, he sued her for divorce.

Frankly, this is folklore in the divorce business. I do not know if this story is true or not; it has nevertheless been told and retold with the names of the people provided. However, because one of my goals in this book is to not get sued, I omit those names here.

Nevertheless, when I am faced with a party seeking such a self-terminating prenup, I tell them by having such a clause in their prenup they are essentially *"buying a divorce"* in ten years' time (or however long they want the clause to be). I tell them this story.

No one ever insisted on such a self-termination clause after hearing this.

Had someone insisted, I would have provided them with the old CYA letter for them to sign. Cover Your Ass. I would have provided them with a letter stating what I advised, what they wanted, and that I included the language over my objection.

This is because there is always the possibility of the client later Blaming Bloom for their predicament.

———

THOSE, OF COURSE, ARE THE EXCEPTIONS.

Representation of a party in a prenup is limited in time duration and involves happy people.

Because of this, such representation is usually more fun than the battlefield of contested divorce litigation.

It is, quite frankly, a good short-term respite from the hand-to-hand combat of a high-conflict divorce.

CHAPTER 10
THE OFFICE WIFE

When running one's own business, including a law firm, it is essential to have appropriate support staff. By that I mean a competent secretary.

The secretary is not merely a typist. She (or he) does far more than that.

A lawyer can, of course, do his/her own typing; and that can be an effective way for self-editing the most complex of legal position papers. When I first came to Ira's office, I handwrote everything before giving it to a secretary to type. One of the skills that I learned during my time with Ira was the use of dictating machines. This made the initial draft of a motion or brief much more time-efficient; and it made the transcription process much easier for the typist – after all, I thought faster than I wrote and almost only slightly faster than I could talk; and my voice was easier to decipher than my handwriting. Of course, while with Ira, we used reel-to-reel machinery and did not utilize microcassettes until I left his employ. More sophisticated equipment arrived years later.

It also does not hurt to have your secretary be both better looking than the lawyer and a nicer and more patient person than the lawyer.

The secretary is the lawyer's gatekeeper. She learns very quickly when to put a call through and when to handle the caller herself.

Over the years, I was blessed with two such women in my life. Actually, Ira was blessed with one and I was so blessed with the other.

———

WAY BACK IN JULY OF 1980, when I went to work for Ira, he had a secretary that I will now call "Betty." Betty was drop-dead gorgeous, a statuesque brunette who could and did charm anyone and everyone. She was so nice that the clients almost always preferred speaking with her than with Ira or me.

Betty could also type faster and more accurately than just about anyone I have ever met.

Betty was so good at her job that she dictated her own hours, preferring to come in around lunchtime and leave in the early evening.

She was an expert at diverting the client from demanding to immediately be put on the telephone with the lawyer she was calling. She was also always professional and, while nice and polite, never once hinting that there was anything other than a very firm line between her and the lawyer (or between her and anyone else for that matter) that would never be crossed. Betty, then in her early 30s, was married to a fireman who was as good-looking as she was.

Did I mention she was beautiful?

When I first met Betty, I was a single 26-year-old man. Other than my new career as a practicing lawyer, I had one thing on my mind which was the social life I had placed on the backburner while attending school.

Indeed, at the end of every business day, Betty would witness the exact same exchange between Ira and myself:

Ira: *Where are you sleeping tonight?*

Me: *None of your f-ing business!*

Ira: *But I need to be able to reach you if I have to.*

Me: *I have an answering machine; and I check it regularly from wherever I am. If you need me, I will call you back.* (In 1980, the closest thing to a cell phone was the shoe phone Maxwell Smart had in the sitcom Get Smart from the 1960s.)

While I had taken note of her beauty, I very quickly looked past that particularly because of her mien and because I then had a very active social calendar.

Betty and I became friends, not merely work colleagues. But that did not stop Betty from expressing her displeasure with my proclivities as a single professional in his late 20s.

I often received calls in the office from women that I was dating. Betty knew our client list, knew that any female lawyer calling me would usually reference the case upon which she was calling, and knew when the caller was neither client nor counsel. On those occasions, I would hear a judgmental tone while being advised that I had a call.

On one occasion, Betty told me, with an attitude, knowing that we had neither a client nor an adversary with that name, *"There's a 'Jennifer House' on the phone for you."* I took the call and spoke for several minutes before returning to Betty's desk to say, *"Thanks. That was about my new couch. It's being delivered on Monday."* Jennifer House was the name of the furniture chain that later became Jennifer Convertibles.

In another instance, a dozen roses were delivered to the office.

The roses were for ME. They were from someone that I was not particularly interested in seeing again; and I wound up giving the roses to Ira to take home to his wife, telling him that "*SOMEBODY should be happy about the roses.*"

The someone was definitely *not* Betty. Indeed, she walked around the office in a funk for hours.

When I finally pressed her on demeanor, I learned that during Betty's entire life – not working life, but her ENTIRE life – whenever there was a delivery of flowers to where she was, those flowers were without fail delivered *for* Betty.

Years later, I am engaged to be married. At the end of one day, my bride-to-be came to the office to pick me up for whatever plans we had for the evening. Betty left an indelible impression on my fiancée.

Fiancée: *Why didn't you tell me she was so beautiful?*

Me: *Because she types 110 words per minute.* [Back then, "words per minute" was a really big deal. I wonder when that no longer became a thing and why. But I digress.]

Fiancée: *But she's gorgeous.*

Me: *But she types 110 words per minute.*

I don't know if she ever got over how attractive Betty was.

———

Fast forward several years.

I was a newlywed, married to the then-fiancée. Ira and I have parted company; and I was in the office provided to me by Ira's friend who had taken me in with an offer that was too good to refuse.

This other lawyer had a morning secretary and a separate afternoon secretary.

Because I was doing virtually all of the legal paperwork, my dictation was the great bulk of the papers to be typed; and as my own personal work grew over time, so, too, did my use of the secretaries' time.

Shortly after coming to this office, the afternoon secretary left for another job. In her place came "Veronica". When the afternoon secretary left, Veronica came in to fill that role.

Veronica was equally attractive as Betty – not statuesque and not brunette, but rather an adorable redhead who dressed in heels so high it was a wonder she could stand at all. She was no less beautiful than Betty. Subjectively – and physical attraction is nothing if not subjective – Veronica was more my type, far more than Betty.

Veronica was also a decade and a half younger than me as compared with my being about half that amount younger than Betty. In fact, when she interviewed with the boss, she lied about her age, claiming to be a few weeks shy of her 18th birthday when she was actually not quite 17 (which we all did not learn until years later).

There is of course no requirement that a secretary be pretty, but it sure didn't hurt, considering that roughly half the clients were men becoming single again.

Veronica and I became fast friends, probably because I made incessant comments about her stiletto heels. I probably could not have gotten away with such jokes today, during the "Me Too" era, but this was the middle of the 1980s. Fortunately, the remarks were taken with the fun that had been intended.

I should mention that many years later, when I closed one of my New York offices and moved to another (and years after Veronica had moved on), I found an old shoe box in the bottom drawer of Veronica's desk. When I called her to see if she wanted me to return the shoes that she had apparently forgotten about at the time she left my employ, I could not help but ask her again, *"How did you ever walk in those things?!?"* At Veronica's instruction, those shoes went directly into the garbage.

At some point, I became too big for my britches in the office of Ira's friend, forcing me to leave and find an office of my own.

At that time, I was compelled to serve as my own office wife, answering my own phone and doing all my own typing. While I became quite good at typing, developed more of an ability to think on the fly, and could edit very efficiently, the extra time involved in preparing paperwork in this fashion was neither cost-effective nor the best use of my time.

Most importantly, there was no buffer between me and the outside world.

But, I was newly married with a brand-new baby at the time, and I no longer had a boss or a sponsoring lawyer who was paying my rent and other office expenses. I was pinching pennies.

Needless to say, this got old for me very quickly. Indeed, the lack of having someone to shield me from clients and other lawyers proved insurmountable.

Although years had passed since we last shared an office, I called Veronica to pull her out of retirement. Veronica had also left that office to have two babies of her own (by then, I, too, had a young son to go with my daughter).

Thankfully, she was willing to have the diversion from full-time mothering; and we arrived at a work schedule that met her parenting demands as well as providing her avoidance of rush hour travel.

———

THE MORNING OF SEPTEMBER 11TH, 2001, was one that no one will ever forget.

The day started with such promise, with the sky being an absolutely gorgeous shade of blue.

As we all now know, the promise of the day turned into a

nightmare, particularly for those of us working in Lower Manhattan.

I was driving across the George Washington Bridge from New Jersey into the City when the second plane hit the World Trade Center. Reports following the striking of the first plane into the Towers had been misreported as being a small plane accident. The smoke that came out of the second Tower, obvious to all on the GW Bridge, left no doubt as to the ominous nature of the events being witnessed.

Veronica, then working mornings, was coming out of the North Tower of the Trade Center, having taken the PATH train into Manhattan from New Jersey.

Virtually all communications went down. Veronica could not reach anyone on the phone – not her family, not me, not anyone. The only telephone call that she made that was able to get through was to my home number, with my wife answering.

My wife was able to reach me on my cell phone, telling me that Veronica was in the middle of the mess downtown, and that, *"she's hysterical,"* before adding, *"I want you to come home now!"*

"You just told me she is hysterical," I replied. *"She's my responsibility! I'm not going to just leave her there!"*

The next two hours were a nightmare.

I exited the Bridge and decided that the Harlem River Drive/FDR Drive was the preferable route to the West Side Highway that I ordinarily used to commute when driving into the office. On this Harlem River/FDR, because of the lack of traffic lights on that eastern route, I sped along with all forms of emergency services until the police directed passenger cars off the highway at the 34th Street exit. But both unclosed and unmanned was the 33rd Street entrance back on the highway; and I took it. I was undisturbed as I continued with only emergency vehicles until the Brooklyn Bridge/City Hall exit, the exit closest to my office and closest to the World Trade Center.

Foregoing a search for a legal parking spot, I created my own in a space under the overpass of the exit I had just taken. I ran the half mile or so to the office. By then, the first Tower had collapsed; downtown Manhattan had literally become a war zone. A cloud of dust was enveloping the atmosphere. Injured people were everywhere, bleeding and worse. I frantically ran past them, barely registering the mayhem around me, because I did not know where the "hysterical" Veronica was. I repeatedly attempted calling her, but by then all cell service had become completely down.

I took the elevator to the 12th floor to my office. Veronica was not there. One of my subtenants was in the office, working, if you can believe it. He had not seen Veronica.

"You gotta get out of here! It's not safe!" I convinced him to leave the office with me immediately. On the elevator ride back to the lobby – and why I chose to use an elevator that morning going either up or down is a mystery – the second Tower collapsed, causing a complete power outage.

The two of us were stuck in the elevator, requiring building maintenance to pry open the doors to the elevator, with our elevator car being frozen between the lobby and the second floor, to allow us to crawl out to relative safety.

Outside on the streets of Lower Manhattan, the collapse of the Second Tower caused an even darker and denser cloud of debris to fill the air. We stayed in the lobby until we could see outside more than a foot or two in front of us.

My subtenant walked home across the Brooklyn Bridge while I continued my desperate search for Veronica, eventually returning to my car in order to cover more ground quickly as I proceeded north. By then, the bridges and tunnels leading out of Manhattan to the north and east to Brooklyn, as well as to the west to New Jersey, had been completely shut down to vehicular traffic, leaving the only option of driving north to the more residential neighborhoods of Manhattan.

I never did find Veronica on the streets of the City, but we were finally able to speak via cell phone. By that time, she was safely ensconced on the Upper East Side in her sister's apartment. My brother was also then living in a rental on the Upper East Side; and we agreed that the four of us would meet for lunch after we both cleaned up.

I arrived at my brother's apartment, my brother, whom I had not seen for a while, greeted me with, *"Larry, you got so gray!"*

"That's not gray! That's the building!"

I showered and borrowed some clean clothing; and we then met Veronica and her sister for lunch.

The difference between Lower Manhattan and the Upper East Side was the difference between war-torn Beirut and Mardi Gras in Rio or New Orleans. The thick, dark cloud downtown was replaced with bright blue skies. The turmoil and desperation of the war zone were replaced with a party.

Veronica and I were astounded by the distinction of where we were from and where we had just been. Despite our descriptions, our siblings could not comprehend the extent of the destruction we had just seen.

———

YEARS LATER, I was representing a client who had come back to my office with a child support enforcement issue arising out of the divorce that I had resolved for her a decade before.

As our initial Court date approached on the following Wednesday, her husband's lawyer was replaced by another lawyer with whom I had a long-time relationship and whom I considered to be a friend.

On the Friday before the appearance in Court, he quite

reasonably asked me for a short adjournment to familiarize himself with the case.

There was no doubt in my mind that such a postponement would be automatically granted; and I had no reason to deny the request.

However, I had a personal issue and told him, *"I'm undergoing shoulder surgery on Monday. If you take care of the adjournment, you have my consent. Tell the judge that I will be home recovering from surgery."*

"No problem."

Or at least we thought there would be no problem.

Wednesday morning, my adversary appeared before the Judge who was not merely newly assigned to this case, but had been newly appointed to the Bench.

He would control his calendar; *not the lawyers!*

The Judge called the office – not his law assistant or other member of his staff – and spoke with Veronica.

By this time, Veronica had been a legal secretary for at least twenty years. But somehow, he said something to Veronica that got her to lower the shield between me and the outside world and tell him my home phone number.

The Judge then called me. Groggily, and fully under the influence of painkillers, I answered. *"Mr. Bloom, unless you are on your deathbed, I expect you in my courtroom at two o'clock."*

What could I do? I could not shower; my left arm was taped to my torso to diminish the chance of injury. I had not shaved since sometime the week before surgery.

I put on a pair of jeans and found the largest shirt that I owned, buttoning it up as much as I could around the arm that could not possibly fit through a sleeve; I put on moccasin shoes that required no tying. I headed first to the office (where I expressed my displeasure to Veronica in no uncertain terms –

probably the only fight we ever had) to get copies of my file; and then I went to Court.

The Judge again ranted about how it was "his" courtroom and that the lawyers could not simply agree to change "his" calendar. He also insisted that I, as the attorney who brought the motion then before him, proceed to argument immediately.

Even though I described for the record my physical appearance, the medications I was on, and the fact that I was *"high as a kite,"* the Judge demanded that I address the merits of my motion. He even refused to accept my statement that *"It would be malpractice for me to argue this motion."*

After a brief whisper at counsel's table with my client, who confirmed that she trusted me, I stated on the record, "I am withdrawing my motion without prejudice to renew." This meant that we would not be proceeding at that time because there was nothing left before the Judge, but that we had the right to bring on the same motion again in the future.

As we left the courtroom, I gave my best, *"I'll be back."*

The following week, I brought the same motion with a short preliminary explanation about what had occurred in Court, and two weeks later, when that motion was heard, we obtained the necessary relief.

———

VERONICA and I have now known each other for almost three-quarters of her life and well over half of mine. Never more than a few months go by without one of us calling the other to catch up.

I have known Veronica during her single days, throughout her marriage, and as the mother of small, though now adult, children. Veronica has known me throughout my marriage, during my divorce, and in my new long-term relationship. Indeed, I was honored to have her sit to my right, with my girlfriend to my left, at my daughter's wedding reception. (My ex was at another table on the other side of the room. That is a story for another book.)

Upon my retirement, it was only Veronica who expressed concern. Not about me, but for herself. To quell her fears, I promised to *"come out of retirement"* if she ever needed my services should she require a divorce.

Over the years that we have known each other, Veronica has referred friends and family to my practice.

If it was even possible, Veronica was better at shielding the boss (then, me) from intrusive phone calls from demanding clients than Betty had been. She engaged each client, explaining that I was tied up, but still getting the reason for the call. This allowed me to analyze the particular issue and arrive at a course of action to meet the client's needs before returning the call or having Veronica return the call.

The truth is that divorce clients are often demanding and almost always needy.

Veronica had far more patience than I could ever expect to possess.

One client was a woman who truly had been the victim of domestic abuse. Her husband had repeatedly beaten her with a belt to the point where the client incurred irreparable facial and vocal disfigurement. She had no one. She made multiple calls to the office daily, and it was impossible to get her off the phone. We were apparently the only people that would speak with her. I could only take so much; and when I explained how expensive it was for her to treat me as her psychotherapist – for which I had absolutely no training – Veronica would speak with her for some-times as much as an hour at a time.

———

Both Betty and Veronica (you guessed it, not their real names) were the perfect office wives. They protected me from intrusions that would have butchered my productivity; they made sure I ate (which, when I was in "the zone," was quite often); they typed like demons; they did not question or challenge the tasks they were assigned nor the reasons for them.

I owe so much to each of them.

And like a real wife, there was no sex between either of them and me.

CHAPTER 11
JUDGES

Yes, Judges are people too.

To say the least, they are very busy people.

On most days, Judges in the Supreme Court are juggling a dozen different cases on their calendar, some with *pro se* litigants (parties without lawyers) but most with two lawyers on a case.

The Family Court Judge may have twenty to forty cases on his/her docket for any given day. In Family Court, the Judge hears cases of custody and support, as well as paternity matters, abuse and neglect, family offenses (also known as domestic violence), and even adoptions but not divorces or property distribution. More often than not at least one of the parties on each case is representing him/herself; and often both.

The job of the Judge hearing a matter with a *pro se* litigant is far more difficult than that of an advocate attorney facing an unrepresented party. (Although it is never easy to be pitted against a self-represented litigant.) The Judge views the matter with fundamental fairness to each side and makes sure that the party without counsel gets a fair shake, while still admonishing the litigant that the rules of evidence apply equally to both sides.

I am often asked by colleagues about particular situations that they are experiencing – usually prefacing any opinion with a question about which side "we" represent. Most recently, I was presented with a set of facts where a party (the other side in my friend-colleague's case) had fired his lawyer and was acting on his own lawyer. In this instance, the Judge crossed the line to such a degree that it was difficult to determine whether he was the Judge or an attorney for the unrepresented husband. My initial response was, *"He can't do that! He has to be off the case!"* We discussed alternative methods to accomplish this before we agreed on which option was optimal. [This is the way I want to spend my retirement – addressing legal issues without having to deal with Judges, clients, or opposing lawyers. Two lawyer friends still call from time to time to "pick my brain;" and I absolutely love it. While I have been trying to get both to retire, I will miss their calls about their pending cases.]

Judges should, and almost always do, provide the unrepresented spouse with a limited adjournment to secure counsel of his/her own. Indeed, failure to do so or to offer an adjournment for this purpose opens any determination subject to reversal on appeal.

There is also something called a judicial temperament. I have always been smart enough to know that I lacked that quality; and I have never even considered seeking a judgeship, notwithstanding my sincere belief that matrimonial judges who were once in the battleground themselves practicing in family law were the most pragmatic and, when necessary, the most decisive. I have always been and always will be an advocate, seeking the optimum resolution for my client. Of course, getting to that best possible result requires knowledge of what would constitute a "fair" resolution of the issues to properly advise the client about what a Judge "might do" if the matter were tried to a decision.

A non-lawyer would truly be surprised at the great number of Judges who avoid rendering a decision.

Every Judge wants the case before him or her to settle. That goes without saying. However, the lack of effort some Judges make towards getting a settlement is not only surprising but also counterproductive as this lack of effort often leads to more work for the Judge in the form of a time-consuming trial and the work of writing a decision after trial.

But Judges do want to settle because Judges have bosses and Judges are themselves judged based on the movement of the caseload. A case that is resolved quickly is a feather in their caps. I said before that Judges are people. While the typical State Court judge has a sense of humor; they each run their courtrooms in their own particular styles.

But cases that don't settle need to be tried; and those cases need to be decided.

Getting to the trial, trying the case, and obtaining a decision takes time, sometimes years; and always exponentially increasing legal fees are charged because of delay.

There are limits on what you can say – and when I once began a reference to the impending reassignment of the judge with the phrase, *"word on the street is..."* – I realized I had gone over the line.

Live and learn. Blame Bloom.

In later years, when I ventured out with my own practice and, for a short period, devoted a small amount of my practice to matters other than family law, including forays before the Federal Court (hence my admissions to the Federal Courts). Although I never took on a Federal appeal (I had obtained admissions to those federal appellate tribunals as prophylactic measures just in case an appeal might become necessary including my admission to the United States Supreme Court in the event that New York's highest court ruled on interpretation of an international treaty thus requiring the "loser" to seek the ultimate interpretation in Washington), I did spend some time before the Federal Trial Bench. For someone like me, more reliant on my sense of humor than are most attorneys, the Federal Court was not the place to me. *They make you act like a lawyer in Federal Court.*

I also learned that appellate practice was an essential part of the contested matrimonial practice.

There are lots of Counties in the State of New York; and I would later learn that there were several, albeit not as many, Counties in the State of New Jersey.

Each County has its own trial level Courts. In New York, for the Family Law practitioner, those are the Supreme Court and the Family Court. As noted, the Family Court can hear custody and support issues (as well as adoptions, paternity cases, and child neglect and abuse matters) but it is without the power/jurisdiction to grant divorces or property distribution. To get that relief, you need the Supreme Court, which has the requisite jurisdiction; and the Supreme Court remains powerless to affect a property distribution unless and until the Court grants the divorce. (Interestingly, despite the "general jurisdiction" of the Supreme Court, it is without jurisdiction to grant an adoption. Adoptions are usually before the Family Court, although the Surrogate Court has adoption jurisdiction as well, even though the Surrogate Court is best known for cases involving estates of the deceased.)

It was for that reason, that the now-abandoned old law for only fault-based divorces was such a valuable tool for the serious matrimonial attorney.

In any event, in addition to the trial-level Courts, there is the appellate judiciary. In both New York and New Jersey, there are two levels of appeals. If you or the other side is unhappy with a ruling, you go to the Appellate Division (same name in each State) even though the ability to get to the initial appeal varies between the two States in which I devoted my professional career.

Although there is an Appellate Division in New Jersey (just one, to which all appeals from every County are heard), there are four Judicial Departments of the Appellate Division in New York handling the appeals from the various Counties. In New York, those Departments are geographically constructed. The First Department hears only appeals from Manhattan and the Bronx; and the Second Department hears the balance of "down State," meaning the other three counties or Boroughs of New York City, the Long Island Counties, and the northern New York City suburbs. (The Third and Fourth Departments are upstate; and far too distant for me to appear – although the Third Department is located in Albany, where New York's highest court, the Court of Appeals, is also located; and I have had matters before the Court of Appeals.)

In New York, it is a fairly easy process (at least in terms of the power/jurisdiction of the Court to hear your appeal) and certainly easier than it is in New Jersey. In New York, there is a right for the loser at the trial level to take an appeal, whereas there is a considerable amount of discretion in terms of taking on an appeal enjoyed by the New Jersey Appellate Division. Furthermore, in New York, if a litigant is (or feels he/she is) aggrieved by an interim determination of the trial-level Court, there is an avenue for interlocutory appellate review, whereas in New Jersey, it is nearly impossible to get that appellate consideration before a final determination is rendered before the Trial Court.

An interesting distinction between decisions from the Appellate Divisions in the two States is whether the decision would appear in the officially published court reporters -- in other words, whether a particular decision will be in the books and available to be utilized as a precedent in future cases. In New York, every appellate determination is officially reported. In New

Jersey, the Appellate Division itself rules on whether the decision on the particular matter before it is to be published or non-published. Indeed, in one of my New Jersey appeals, the Appellate Division, while marking the matter as unpublished, did refer the issue determined therein to the committee responsible for promulgating the Court Rules for the purpose of establishing a new Court Rule that addressed the issued it had decided against my client but still elected not to publish.

Each of these States has another level of appellate practice in the form of its highest Court. In New York, that is called the Court of Appeals (confusing because that is what the mid-level Federal Court is called); and in New Jersey, that is called the Supreme Court (just like the United States Supreme Court is the federal court of ultimate authority, as distinguished from New York's trial-level Supreme Court – making matters really confusing).

I have had cases in the two downstate New York appellate departments as well as the Court of Appeals. After "the break-up" with Ira, I expanded my practice to New Jersey (having gained admission to the Bar of that State by passing the Bar Exam shortly after my marriage and almost five years following law school and my initial Bar Exam in New York) and handled cases before that State's Appellate Division.

The Courts make the law; but my cases have certainly had a hand in formulating new legal doctrine. I have never made new law, but several of my cases provided the factual background for that law as well as some of my arguments have been adopted as rationale for such a change. Some of those determinations went my way; others did not. One of those cases made new law even though neither lawyer argued for it. (It became an ongoing joke that opposing counsel and I for years to come that we had a case that created a particular legal precedent even though neither of us had raised the question at either the trial or the appellate level.)

As but a single example, I represented in New Jersey a man who owned a 1% share in a closed, non-public corporation. We disclosed the name of the corporation, the minimal value we believed my client's interest was worth as well as the debt in the same amount that supported his acquisition of his ownership interest, the sum of $17,000. The case proceeded; and we eventually settled with everyone being happy about the resolution. But then my client acted in a way that proved the adage that you are never really divorced after the judgment of divorce and that the parties still had to deal with each other. He started a spending spree, which included the purchase of a very large house that he bought without a mortgage (a mortgage is a public record easily found; the lack of any such record of a mortgage was easily identified), as well as the purchase of a four-karat diamond ring for his new trophy wife. The first wife discovered these purchases, which was not too difficult since my guy picked up the parties' children for visitation with the trophy wife and her sparkling finger, and then spent his time with the children at his new house.

How could he afford it? Well, the closed corporation had gone "public" before the divorce agreement, and was publicly listed on one of the principal stock exchanges; the $17,000 interest (backed by the $17,000 debt that we had also previously disclosed) suddenly became worth $1.6 Million. The first wife found herself a new lawyer who sued the now ex-husband, seeking to reopen the financial issues of the basis of fraud. The client returned to me who had obtained a far better settlement than the facts (undisclosed even to me) would have warranted. We argued that we disclosed the interest in the business and that it was the Wife's original lawyer's obligation to do his due diligence to obtain a proper evaluation of the business. In short, we argued that we had done nothing wrong and that the first lawyer had committed legal malpractice by failing to do his homework. The trial-level

Court agreed with me and dismissed the application to set aside the financial terms of the divorce.

Not satisfied, the first wife hired yet another lawyer to file an appeal; and again, I appeared on behalf of the husband, renewing the arguments that had been accepted by the Court below. The three-judge panel, one of whom had previously sat as the Presiding Family Part Judge in my home county, heard oral argument; and it was the proverbial "hot Bench." They wanted to know the timing of the initial public offering on the corporation; they wanted to know who knew what and when – including me; and in the immortal words of Sergeant Schultz, *"I knew nothing."* The Appellate Division reversed the lower court and remanded the matter back to the initial court for more proceedings. My client then hired another lawyer; and I lost contact with the case. He clearly Blamed Bloom for the ramifications of his own actions rather than recognizing the ramifications of his actions.

The foregoing was the case where the New Jersey Appellate Division elected not to publish its ruling but did go further by referring to the State Committee on Judicial Rules. A few months after the appellate determination, a brand-new Court Rule was issued and made part of the public record, providing that whenever a substantial change to the value of an asset occurred during the pendency of a divorce case, it was the affirmative obligation of the party with knowledge of the change to disclose that change in circumstance. In other words, the argument that once a disclosure of an asset was made, it was incumbent upon the other side to disclose major changes to its value.

ANOTHER OF MY NEW JERSEY divorce cases was almost as noteworthy.

I represented the friend and client of one of my neighbors. I obtained a divorce for him with very favorable results. In fact, at the end of the case, he insisted that we share victory cigars. That cigar was the last cigar I ever had as I developed a distaste for them following further events in the litigation that I had thought I had successfully concluded.

After the wife had been represented by a small town firm that could essentially have been called "Frick & Frack, Attorneys at Law," lawyers that could have written the book on lawyer incompetence, the now ex-wife had a change of heart and decided to consult with one of the big-name New Jersey matrimonial attorneys (with whom I was aware because my college and law school roommate had a wife with whom he would eventually go to trial and appeal that was represented by the same named attorney).

Somehow, this shyster (which I guess tells you, the reader, what I think of him) convinced my client's ex-wife to reopen the divorce claiming that she had Battered Wife Syndrome.

They claimed that a pattern of physical and sexual abuse left the wife unable to give *bona fide* consent.

This case exemplifies the old adage that appearances can be deceiving.

The husband and wife were both short, dumpy people. Neither was particularly attractive or noteworthy to any degree. Looking at them, one assumed they had a vanilla lifestyle.

However, after a discussion with my client, I learned how wrong I could be. Our defense to the allegations of domestic violence was that the physicality was part of the role-play sexual fantasy in which the parties engaged. In other words, the physical and sexual allegations were, in fact, consensual.

My client brought me books in which the parties each made handwritten notations in preparation for their own role-playing sex. Those books and the notes in them were introduced into evidence at trial with graphic testimony from my client. My use of these books on cross-examination of the wife was met with denials, although I was able to get her to admit to the identity of the writer of each handwriting sample – some of which were her husband's and some of which were her own. She just refused to acknowledge that this was a prop, script, or how-to manual concerning the sex life of the parties during their marriage.

We won the trial, but lost on appeal when the wife changed attorneys yet again, using the services of one of the most respected matrimonial attorneys in the State in his last case before taking the Bench (and who shortly thereafter was elevated to the Appellate Division, becoming one of the youngest to ever sit on that Court).

CHAPTER 12
JUDGES (PEOPLE REALLY)
SAY THE DARNEDEST THINGS

THE JUDGE that heard the aforementioned "small tushie" case was someone I had known for a long time. Indeed, the way I described it to opposing counsel on another case was that *"I've known her since I called her by her first name."* After she took the Bench, it was always "Your Honor" or "Judge."

She had been friends with Ira; and when Ira wasn't available to answer her questions (she was a new lawyer at the time, having attended law school during the time she served as a Court Officer in the Family Court), I was able to help her. We became friends.

I still quote her, years after her retirement from the Bench, for one of her tried and true remarks: *"Elephants don't marry giraffes."*

When a husband or wife has a character defect, his/her spouse may have the same defect or an equally unattractive dissimilar character defect. It is the equivalent of me saying to a client, *"You married him"* or *"You married her."*

After the "small tushie" case, I was before this same Judge on another matter. But I was late for Court thanks to the reliability of the New York City Subway System. Rather than being chastised for my tardiness as any other judge would have done, this judge actually said on the record, *"Mr. Bloom, you're late. You're never late. We were worried about you."*

The lawyer on the other side, a woman of about my age with whom I was cordial, stopped me outside the courtroom after this exchange.

"Boy, the Judge really likes you."

"I know. I've known her a long time, since before she took the Bench."

"Did you sleep with her?"

I was confounded by this; but responded without filter, *"Don't be silly. If I slept with her, she would have had to recuse herself."*

My adversary then transformed herself into a contestant on *Who Wants to Be a Millionaire?* Talk about no filters! She verbalized her thought process, pointing at various points in the area, going, *"Recuse ... recuse ... recuse,"* indicating all of the attorneys with whom she had had sex. She also made clear that I could be included in that "recusal list," with me demurring with a *"when the case is over"* remark. When the case concluded, I did not pursue that proposition.

———

ONE MORNING, I was before a Judge in a County in the middle of New Jersey to argue a motion. The Judge indicated that he would hear my case on "second call," meaning that I had to wait for oral argument while the Judge attended to other cases on the calendar.

I explained that my appearance was required that afternoon at 2:00 p.m. in a Court north of New York City.

"How fast do you drive?" the Judge asked.

"As fast as the law allows," I responded.

This got me a laugh from the assembled lawyers awaiting the

call of their own cases as well as getting my point across to the Judge.

———

I REPRESENTED A WOMAN in what originally looked like it might go on for a very long time since her husband was angry and would not agree to anything.

We ultimately resolved the factual issues.

Then came the time for the divorce itself. The contested divorce became uncontested, which is the desire in all marital litigation.

But there were catches.

First, this was a New Jersey divorce; and the pre-pandemic procedure State-wide was for personal appearances where the parties each usually testified as to the fairness of and their consent to their agreement, and then at least one of them testified to the facts underlying their claim (or "cause of action") for divorce. [During the pandemic, some (but not all, of the New Jersey Courts, expanded their procedures to allow for video appearances – and some even allowed for "submission divorces" where no one appeared, and testimony came utilizing sworn affidavits. New York was, is, and probably always will be a submission State as regards most uncontested divorces, with only a few contest-becoming-uncontested matters processed the personal appearance route.]

The benefit of the New Jersey pre-pandemic procedure was that the clients each walked out of Court holding a certified copy of the final Judgment of Divorce. The case was over. If they wanted, they could get married the next day.

In this particular case, that was both a very good thing and a very bad thing.

My client was nine months pregnant with her boyfriend's

baby at the time. In fact, when I saw her that morning, she told me that she was already two centimeters dilated, with the birth being imminent.

Good: she would at least be divorced when she gave birth; and, with a little bit of luck, she might even get to be married to the baby's father before birth, or at the very least shortly thereafter.

So, what could be bad? Well, hubby had no idea that his wife was even pregnant. We had no idea what he would do when he saw his wife's physical condition. The divorce and the underlying agreement might well have been in jeopardy.

Fortunately, I was able to convince the husband's lawyer (who also wanted no more problems in the case and desired the expedited conclusion thereof) that he communicates with his client, telling him that there was no need for his personal appearance as the lawyer could take care of everything without him.

We all (except the husband) arrived early in Court on the morning that the case appeared on the uncontested calendar.

While waiting, the Judge came out of his Chambers -- apparently his secretary or court officer passed on their observations as to the size of my client's belly. *"Mr. Bloom, can we speak for a minute?"*

The answer to that question is never "No." *"Of course, Your Honor,"* and I step outside.

"Where are you on the calendar?"

"Number 7, Your Honor."

"No! You are now number 1! And get her out of here as fast as you can!!!"

We complied; and they all lived happily ever after.

———

JUDGES, too, have had very funny things to say both in the area of recusal and just in general.

On one occasion, I represented a urologist in his divorce case. His case was called on a large calendar day when the courtroom was packed before a single Judge who ascertained the trial readiness of all the cases and then assigned the cases that were ready to go to other Judges on specific days. Before either lawyer could give his appearance (name, address, and the party whom we represent), the Judge called the two lawyers up to the Bench for an informal discussion off the record. At the Bench, the Judge whispered that he needed to recuse himself from our case. Never being the shy one, I inquired as to why. The Judge then announced to the two lawyers, *"Mr. Bloom, your client did my vasectomy."*

That was sufficient to have the matter reassigned immediately, not to mention being sufficient to redden my face.

———

THERE WERE ALSO OCCASIONS where I represented people who later became judges.

Often, when my former clients were on the Bench, I would have a case randomly assigned to these client-judges.

Obviously, this presented an impermissible conflict of interest. The Judge whom I had represented could not sit in judgment on one of my cases. Recusal was a given.

One would think that there would be no problem with this; but there was an issue about how the conflict would be presented to the parties and opposing counsel as well as how it would appear on the record.

Certainly, there was a client confidentiality that needed to be honored. I could not say that *"I represented his [or her] Honor,"* because that was protected confidentiality; and it was unlikely that the Judge would reveal in open court anything about his [or her] own divorce. Nor would I lie by saying that the Judge had represented me.

I was able to diffuse this issue by indicating that *"before the Judge took the Bench, a lawyer-client relationship existed between us."* This was vague enough that it could have been concluded that the Judge in question had represented me and equally vague that the prior representation was related to something other than a matrimonial. Either reason would have sufficed to have the Judge removed from the matter I was handling.

————

I ALSO APPEARED before a Judge who had previously been an adversary of mine some years before.

Upon my first appearance before her, she immediately recused herself from hearing the case upon which I had come to Court.

I had never represented her, and she had never represented me.

What had occurred was that we were adversaries representing opposing sides on a divorce.

During that earlier matter, a settlement conference took place in my office.

Negotiations had been heated. I eventually kicked both this lawyer and her client out of my office.

This was not an unusual situation. In fact, it was fairly common. (I have a friend whom I had met on a case who told me, *"I remember our first telephone conversation. You hung up on me."* I responded by saying, *"You have to be more specific."*)

Years later, as I stood before the Judge in her Courtroom and heard her recusing herself from involvement in the case on which I appeared, I remembered the incident. Once we were off the record and with the permission of the Judge, I approached the Bench with the other lawyer on the case, indicating off the record to the Judge that there was really no need for the recusal. However, the Judge elected not to hear my case.

I guess that Judge still had a grudge against me from her lawyer days. In retrospect, it was better that she elected to recuse herself.

———

IN ANOTHER INSTANCE, I was representing the wife of a man who owned a majority interest in a car dealership.

The facts were these: The parties were married for 20 years with five children. My client was the stay-at-home mom devoted to her kids. The husband was a drunk devoted to the bottle and his toys one of which was a girlfriend. While often not being able to function, he kept it together enough to grow an extremely successful car dealership.

Every time the case was on, my client and I obtained a win. There were many motions and many rulings by the Court before the time of trial; and each time we were successful.

Then, one day, the husband came into Court with a new lawyer. Before the Judge took the Bench for the day, the Judge came into the Well (the area between the Judge's Bench and where the lawyers sit) and asked to speak with me. He was standing there with the husband's new lawyer when he told me that *"Mr. P is the defendant's new attorney. He's my best friend, and I need to recuse myself from this case."*

My client, the wife, was not far away and heard this exchange, looked over at her, and asked, *"Do you trust me?"* She nodded her head, indicating an affirmative response. I say to the Judge, *"We waive the conflict. There is no need for recusal."*

"Mr. Bloom, you can do anything you want, but he's my best friend, and I am not sitting on this case."

———

ON ANOTHER OCCASION, I was able to use recusal to the client's advantage. One of my friends was representing a man in an upstate County who was having a hard time before the one and only Judge who heard matrimonial cases in that small County.

That Judge had previously been the County Executive of a neighboring county. He was also the ex-husband of one of my former clients.

For this reason alone, I was brought in to replace my friend as the attorney of record for the husband, causing the immediate recusal of the Judge from the matter.

But be careful what you wish for! Or, as I have often said to a client (particularly useful when a father said he wanted custody of his child but was unprepared to actually have custody), *"What happens if you win?"*

They brought in another Judge from another County to hear the smaller upstate County case. This new Judge was someone with whom I had also had a history in his home County, with him adjudicating several of my prior cases; and he was none too happy about having to travel to another County.

During an oral argument on a motion in one of those earlier cases, the Judge became so enraged with the argument I had made and how I made it that he banged his hand on the desk in front of him, hitting a pencil which then flew off his desk, across the Courtroom, striking opposing counsel in the chest. Everyone in the Courtroom, other than the Judge and my adversary, did their best to stifle a laugh.

———

THE JUDGE/FORMER COUNTY EXECUTIVE referenced above had been the defendant-husband in an action that had been commenced by another lawyer that I knew well. That lawyer had offices in the very same County in which the person he was suing was the then-current County Executive. For reasons best known to himself, this lawyer elected to start the divorce action in that same County.

The selection of the venue was questionable. Yes, both parties resided there. However, the statute governing the selection of venue provided for alternatives.

In this case, with both parties residing in the County Executive's County, that County was not objectionable and, thus, an entirely appropriate County in which to litigate this divorce. Indeed, the initial selection of any other County in the State might have resulted in a motion by the husband's lawyer to bring it back to the so-called "proper" County.

Nevertheless, had I been the Plaintiff's original lawyer, I would have taken the risk of facing such a motion and selected any other County in which to litigate that divorce, but I came into the case with it having already been begun by my own client in the home County.

There were several reasons for this. Even though the Judge and the County Executive were in different branches of the government – the Judge being a State employee and the County Executive being a County employee of the executive branch – and thus there was no employer-employee relationship between them, the venue that my predecessor selected was troublesome.

Furthermore, the grounds for divorce that were listed in the Summons for Divorce were also misguided. [It is worth noting that in New York, a divorce case is started with the filing of a Summons (or by the filing of a Summons and Complaint) in the County in which the action is to be brought. The plaintiff then causes the Summons to be served personally upon the Defendant.

The Summons lists in summary fashion the grounds for divorce, usually referencing the applicable paragraph of Section 170 of the Domestic Relations Law and the forms of ancillary relief being requested (such as spousal maintenance and the distribution of marital property, to name but two), without addressing the particular acts of the defendant giving rise to the cause of action (the particular ground for divorce selected) as well as some statutory notices concerning the continuation of all existing insurance and also related to the spousal maintenance guidelines. A formal Complaint for Divorce detailing the grounds referenced summarily in the Summons (itemizing the cruelty, the adultery, and/or abandonment) need not be served with the Summons; and, indeed, there are times when a Complaint is not served for months or even years after the Summons. This is in contrast to New Jersey, where the Complaint is first filed setting forth the detailed alleged misconduct of the defendant; and after filing defendant is personally served with both a Summons and a Complaint.]

The husband then retained two law firms to represent him in the divorce, a well-known politically-connected firm within the County in which the action was pending as well as perhaps the most well-respected matrimonial attorney in the State of New York.

Before I was retained, the matter had been assigned to a Judge; and the matter had been marked "super sealed" and a gag order issued to prevent public discussion relative to this divorce. To this day, I do not know what the term "super sealed" means. All divorce files are "sealed," meaning that only the parties to the divorce themselves, as well as their respective attorneys, have access to the files of the case. This is in contrast to other civil and criminal litigation, the file of which are "public record," access to which is open to the general public.

My acquaintance was in over his head in this politically charged matter in his home County; and he knew it.

I came aboard since I was representing the guy's best friend in a complicated divorce case in the same County.

Upon my discussions with the client, I learned that her husband had a history of dalliances and that he had then had two girlfriends or "paramours." One of those women happened to be the County Attorney of the very same County in which the husband was County Executive.

I also learned from the local media that the Judge assigned to this matter had recently become engaged to marry an Assistant County Attorney in this same County.

In other words, the Judge hearing the divorce case was intimately involved with an underling of a woman alleged to be in an adulterous relationship with the defendant.

This all seemed too incestuous for me; and I truly believed that my client could not obtain a fair trial from this Judge or, indeed, from any Judge in that County.

I considered it then – and I will go to my grave still believing – to reference Shakespeare, that something was rotten in the State of Denmark. In fact, it stunk.

So as the newly retained lawyer #2 for the wife, there was a lot for me to do.

1. I prepared a Complaint for divorce as this case commenced with the service of a Summons only, which listed cruelty and abandonment as the grounds for divorce. I alleged not merely the husband's cruel and inhuman treatment of the wife, listing in detail each act of misconduct over the course of the preceding five years that my client could remember, as well as constructive abandonment (his refusal to engage in sexual relations with his wife for a period of more than a year), but we also specifically as possible set forth each act of adultery with each of the named co-respondents (i.e., para-

mours) of which we were aware along with the catchall "and such other and further times and places more particularly within the knowledge of the Defendant and his paramour(s)." I also prepared a proposed Amended Summons setting forth adultery with a separate cause of action with respect to each of the two women.

2. Next, we brought a motion before the Judge assigned to the case, asking

a. For permission to amend the Summons, to reflect the adultery causes of action, and

b. For recusal of the Judge based upon the "gross" (my word) appearance of impropriety due to his own intimate relationship with the assistant to a named co-respondent in the litigation and

c. For a change of venue to another County because of these issues, as well as the prominence of the Defendant and one of the named Co-Respondents, would render it impossible for my client to obtain a fair trial before any Judge in that County, and

d. For interim financial relief in the form of *pendente lite* spousal maintenance and *pendente lite* counsel fees, as well as

e. For the lifting of the "super seal" and "gag" orders.

The motion was heard in Chambers (the back room behind the public courtroom) so that no one was privy to the arguments other than the Court staff, the parties, and their attorneys. An argument in open Court would have subjected the issues to any other lawyer or litigant (or any member of the public) that may have been in the Courtroom at the time. I did not, and would never have, objected to the argument in Chambers for the simple reasons that I would not have been successful and that I was already on thin ice with this Judge in referencing his own personal life.

Thereafter, in an 81-page single-spaced Decision, the Judge writes *"motion denied,"* all of which was essentially saying, *"I have done nothing wrong and see no reason to recuse myself; and by the way,*

I sanction Mr. Bloom $10,000." That was the maximum financial sanction available under the Court Rules.

I appealed this determination and was able to obtain a reduction of the sanction to only $5,000, which I paid after my application to the Court of Appeals in Albany for leave to file a further appeal[2] was denied. I paid the sanction. Were the matter not so politically charged, I doubt seriously that any financial sanction against me would have been upheld on appeal.

This ruling also created a rift between my client and me; and she soon thereafter moved on to lawyer #3.

As lawyers, we are required to take a certain number of hours each year of continuing legal education, which includes ethics credits.

One such class is an annual class taught by a law professor at my alma mater, who is also a practicing matrimonial attorney. His class was and is a must-attend. Not only is it the most comprehensive review of the relevant case law of the preceding twelve months taught in a highly entertaining manner, but it is also the place to see and be seen, to catch up with former adversaries, to talk settlement with counsel on current cases, and to hang out in an informal setting with Judges who regularly attend to keep current.

Every year, the lecturer gives the same admonition when it comes to recusal: *If you are going to try to kill the King, make sure he's dead!* (I later learned that this had already been referenced by Mr. Nizer in his 1961 book.)

Maybe I should have been a better student.

But I really believed that recusal for this judge would have been a no-brainer.

---

2. In New York, there are only limited instances where a party has a "right" to appeal from the Appellate Division to the Court of Appeals. If the particular case did not fall within the enumerated appeal-as-of-right circumstances – and this case did not, a motion must be made for permission, or "leave," to appeal.

Alas, I was in error, and the King survived if only to punish his attacker.

———

THE ISSUE OF RECUSAL has always been a peculiar one.

There are obvious instances where I previously represented someone who later became a judge or where I had represented the judge's spouse.

Otherwise, the statute relating to recusal only mandates recusal when there exists between the judge and a party a relationship "by consanguinity or affinity," which is just a fancy way of saying "by blood or marriage."

The great bulk of judicial recusals, either on motion of one of the parties or by the Court on its own motion, are relegated to the sound discretion of the Court. This discretion means that the Judge can resolve the issue of whether to stay on the particular case based on whatever the Judge feels is right. The exercise of that discretion is rarely altered by appellate review.

If you are going to try to kill the King, make sure he's dead!

———

BUT RECUSAL IS ALSO waivable (if the Judge consents).

I had an instance in the Family Court where the. support issues were handled by a Support Magistrate [sort of a junior and lesser paid Judge], and custodial issues were handled by a Family Court Judge.

On this particular occasion, both litigations were going on simultaneously often calling for the parties and respective counsel to appear before both a Judge and a Support Magistrate on the same day. (However, bureaucracies being what they are, the cases were sometimes heard on different days which unnecessarily added to the legal fee burden of the parties.)

We appeared before the Support Magistrate who happened to have been a former client of mine. But then, it had been well over ten years since my prior representation of her had concluded. The adversary, whom I had known for decades (as he had started out having worked for a friend and contemporary of Ira Bennett when I started with Ira), had no objection to the Magistrate hearing our case even in the face of my prior representation. The Magistrate was also amenable to hearing the case with this waiver from the other side.

As an aside, we were also before a Judge together with an attorney who had been assigned to represent the children of the parties. While we waiting in the vestibule, the three lawyers were just talking good-naturedly. In fact, I distinctly remember saying to the mother's lawyer, *"Do you remember when we were the youngest lawyers in the Courthouse; and now we are the oldest lawyers here?"* He and I joked with each other and talked about golf. Then, the Judge called us into Chambers where the wife's counsel and I engaged in a true adversarial argument addressing the merits of the case.

After the conference we left Chambers; and the young attorney assigned to represent the children looked at us and expressed amazement that we could be the best of friends in one minute and then be at each other's throats the next.

Unfortunately, the County where I had the recusal motion leading to being sanctioned was a County where I had, for a time, a substantial portion of my clientele. I had been involved with a parents' rights group (ostensibly a women's rights group, but they insisted that they catered to neither gender over the other) in the same County that referred a considerable number of potential clients my way.

That case involving the County Executive, as well as this other case, caused my eventual self-imposed exile from that County.

Before that exile, I represented a husband who was a lawyer. He had a wife and a son; and I do not believe that the wife would have been satisfied even if she were awarded one of my client's testicles.

They fought about everything.

My client became in arrears in his temporary, *pendente lite,* support and counsel fee obligations.

The matter is scheduled on a motion day; and all signs pointed to my client being set up to be taken into custody and jailed for non-payment.

Murphy's Law again: What can go wrong will go wrong.

My home and this Courthouse were separated by a river; and its crossing required the passage over one particular bridge.

Although my habit was to leave enough time for all traffic contingencies, I did not factor in the dump truck that emptied its entire load in the center lane of the bridge I needed to cross, leading me to be two hours late for this appearance.

When I arrived at the Courthouse, my first stop, as a man of a certain age who had been stuck in dead-stop traffic for hours, was to visit the Men's Room.

"Where are you going, Larry?" asked a Court Officer who was well known to me.

"Stuck in traffic. I need the restroom."

"Not yet. The Judge wants you NOW!"

"But …"

"NOW!!!"

As the officer carried a gun, I thought it best to adhere to his request and go immediately into the Courtroom

Before I could sit down or say anything to my client or court personnel, my case was called.

"Note your appearances for the record," said the Judge.

The plaintiff's counsel noted her appearance; and I noted mine. We each indicated our respective names, addresses, and the party that each represented.

Knowing what was going to happen by the presence of four Court Officers in the courtroom and two more just outside the door, I had to distract the Court from its apparent intention to incarcerate my client. While the presence of a Court Officer in the Courtroom has always been established practice, the presence of two was a rarity; and the presence of more than two was unheard of.

As the Judge starts to speak, I interrupt, *"Excuse me, Your Honor, but I note that there are four ARMED[3] Court Officers in this courtroom and two more ARMED Court Officers immediately outside that door."*

"Sit down, Mr. Bloom."

"But I want their appearances in the record."

"Sit down, Mr. Bloom!"

"But Your Honor has created an aura of intimidation; and the record should specifically reflect this."

"I said, sit down, Mr. Bloom!!!"

I persisted. *"That's it,"* sayeth the Judge, slamming his hand on the table; and, then the Judge, pointing to the Officer who had not let me go to the restroom, *"TAKE THAT MAN INTO CUSTODY!"* The Judge then stormed off the Bench into the back room.

I was surrounded by the four guys with guns, the lead one handcuffing in the courtroom before the parties, the other lawyer, the Court staff, and all the other people there for other cases.

"You are hurting me," I protested.

---

3. Of course, all Court Officers are armed. They are: the guys with the guns.

"Shut up! What did you think we would do?"

I was then led to what had been an empty Robing Room, placed in a chair, and told to keep quiet. I was left there still in handcuffs for almost an hour, after which a single Officer came in and said, *"I'll escort you out of the building."*

"But I don't come here very often, and I have other things to do in the building," I tell him.

"Not today!"

"May I at least use the restroom?"

That was allowed; and I was then escorted downstairs and out of the building.

The Judge was not satisfied and issued an Order imposing financial sanctions against me. After I obtained an appellate stay of enforcement of those sanctions, the Judge elected to allow me enough due process to allow me to address him on whether sanctions were appropriate under the circumstances.

In other words, the Judge wanted me to get down on my knees and beg forgiveness, scheduling this appearance on a day when the courtroom would be packed.

Instead of apologizing, I engaged in a filibuster, figuring I had a captive audience behind me. I spoke for 45 minutes, explaining in painstaking detail that my conduct on the day in question was not only unsanctionable but necessary to protect the rights of my client, who had been set up to be arrested.

I was still sanctioned which ultimately was reversed this time on appeal.

But my client was not arrested on that initial appearance; and he went on to fight another day.

As a footnote, a couple of years later, I appeared before another Judge in a further Upstate County having been reassigned from the same County in which I had had all those problems. As we were talking off the record, he asked me if I ever got to the County in which these things happened.

"As a matter of fact, Your Honor, I had been there quite a bit; but I am now persona non grata there."

"Why do you say that?"

I cut to the chase, *"Judge So-and-so had me cuffed."*

He then banged his fist on the table and exclaimed, *"You're the one!"* We then shared a laugh.

I spent a great deal of time thereafter preparing a complaint to sue that Judge, each of the six Court Officers, and the State of New York, for wrongful imprisonment.

I had seriously thought about suing the State of New York, for whom I would have argued that the Judge and his six Court Officers were representatives, as well as the Judge and each such officer in their individual capacities based upon their wrongful detention and wrongful imprisonment of me. I had even drafted a Complaint with which to initiate such a lawsuit.

In New York, there is a special Court with jurisdiction over lawsuits involving the State called the Court of Claims. Usually, a single Judge sits in the Court of Claims in each County of the State of New York.

As luck would have it, the Court of Claims Judge for this particular County was the sister-in-law of my college and law school roommate. I saw her regularly at my friend's home as well as at all of that friend's family functions. Indeed, during my entire career as an attorney, she was the only Judge that I regularly kissed on the cheek when I saw her (though always referring to her as "Your Honor.") Why? Because I never appeared before her and never expected I would ever appear before her.

For this reason and for the reason that I was the party suing (not merely the attorney for the party suing), I believed it prudent to have an independent attorney representing me.

I went to most of the lawyers I knew, each of whom wanted no part in suing a sitting Judge. I had hoped that a friend thirty years my senior, himself then upon the cusp of retirement and without any practice in that County, would agree to be front-man while I ghostwrote the papers; but he also refused.

Eventually, discretion became the better part of valor as I decided that maybe this potential lawsuit was not a wise career move for an aged 40-something litigator still practicing in several other Counties.

———

JUDGES ARE ALSO the masters of their Courtrooms.

I represented a man in a divorce action in a Court located at the edge of my geographic practice area. I did not know the judge before I got involved; in fact, I had never had a case in that particular County.

We were in the middle of the third day of trial when the Judge conferenced the case with the attorneys between witnesses. We were still on the presentation of the case for the Plaintiff-wife; and I had yet to put my client on the witness stand or to present any evidence of our own except for what came out during cross-examination. The Judge wanted to know from the Plaintiff's lawyer who his next witness would be and asked for a proffer of what that testimony would be.

When my adversary indicated that his next witness would be the parties' adult twenty-one-year-old daughter and that the testimony would be about how she had witnessed repeated beatings of her mother by her father, the Judge exploded. *"I don't want a child testifying in my Court. This case is going to settle; and it is going to settle NOW! Mr. Bloom, if I have to hear this evidence, I am going to hold it against YOUR CLIENT! NOW, GO OUTSIDE AND MAKE SURE YOUR CLIENT SETTLES NOW!!!"*

This, of course, absolutely destroyed my negotiating position. But then again, I was not the one who committed domestic abuse in front of his adult child. (Had the child witnessing the violence been under 18, this domestic abuse in and of itself would have been a sufficient basis for my client losing on the issue of custody.)

I went to my client as instructed; and I told him exactly what had transpired in Chambers. I told him he had no choice but to settle, that he had to cut his losses. While I was willing to continue the trial to a conclusion, I advised him that this was a waste of his money and that were he to continue he would be buying himself an appeal. I also discussed with the client the possible disqualification of the witness because domestic violence was not "egregious spousal misconduct" relevant to the issue of property distribution – although the Judge had clearly indicated that he would not go in that direction.

We settled.

This was another instance where the lawyer did not lose the case; the client did.

———

THE ALL-TIME FUNNIEST thing I have ever heard a judge say was unrelated to recusal. I was walking with Ira in the lobby of the Appellate Division, where we ran into one of the newest Judges of that esteemed Court. Ira knew him for many years before he took the Bench, as well as the Judge's Jewish wife. This Judge had just become one of the first African American Judges on the appellate level in the State of New York.

After introducing me, his new associate attorney to the Judge, Ira asked, *"So Judge, how's the new job?"*

The Judge led us to a quiet corner, looked around, and then whispered, *"They got me working like a Schvartze!"* [For the reader not conversant in Yiddish, the term "Schvartze" is a derogatory reference to a Black person.]

CHAPTER 13
STUPID THINGS I'VE SAID

IN ADDITION to saying to a Judge about the rumors concerning her reassignment, and prefacing my remark with the immortal, *"Word on the street, Your Honor, is ..."* I have said things that I would like to have taken back.

As you will recall, the 2000 presidential election involving Al Gore and George W. Bush gave rise to considerable litigation ultimately winding up in the United States Supreme Court.

At a Hanukkah party with my wife's three cousins and their husbands, the cousin who was married to the lawyer (as opposed to the one married to the doctor and the one married to the dentist) approached me.

"I have a connection and may be able to get us both on the legal team relative to the election appeal," he said.

Now, I was not and never would be considered to be an expert on election law; but by the year 2000, I had been an attorney for twenty years with substantial appellate experience. In short, I was an expert in legal research and could write an appellate brief as well as anyone. Indeed, back in the early 1980s, while working for Ira Bennett, we did so much work in the

Appellate Division for the Second Judicial Department located in Brooklyn, that when I walked into the Clerk's Office, I was usually greeted with, *"Hey Larry, what have you got for us today?"*

In any event, being part of a legal team that would undoubtedly make history – both legal history and the history of the United States – was something that was very appealing to me. I was also not averse to "ink" and other publicity.

But it did not end there.

No, stupid me, started asking questions.

"What side are we on?" This is a question that I routinely asked when a divorce case was referred to me or when one of my colleagues sought advice on how to handle a case. My first question when a colleague posed a divorce question to me has always been, *"Do we represent the husband or the wife?"* *"Do we represent the monied or the non-monied spouse?"*

A good lawyer knows how to argue both sides; and I have always been able to do just that. I only need to orient my thinking about which side I am on.

But, in this instance – and now more than two decades later – did it really matter whether I was on the Bush side or the Gore side? It did not; and I should have kept my big mouth shut. I should have had that case, regardless of the side I represented, as part of my professional resume.

Unfortunately, I did not swallow the question.

That election, although only a precursor of what would transpire over the next twenty-plus years, was emotional for the country and emotional for the electorate; and it did matter a great deal to me the side for which I would be working.

"Bush," my cousin replied.

"I was really rooting for the other side on this one." What an idiot I was! As if asking the question wasn't bad enough.

Needless to say, that was the last I ever heard about working on that case.

As a result of my slip of the tongue, whatever legal history I was to make in my legal career would have to be confined to matrimonial matters.

———

Of course, as lawyers we are stuck with our clients and with the facts as they come down the line.

In one instance, I represented an alleged father in a paternity case. It was during the early days of HLA testing and before DNA testing, thus leaving me some room for argument. The HLA test controlled the determination of paternity.

During my 40+ years in family law, the science of paternity law has matured, and the law has changed dramatically, albeit with time lags.

When I was still working for Ira, and we had the entertainer who had fathered our client's child, the legal standard was "opportunity, inclination, and intent." In other words, there was no science involved in identifying a father. As I noted previously, the existing science was in the form of blood typing and could only be legally used to exclude a potential father. (If the child was Type A and the mother was Type A, an alleged father with Type B blood could not scientifically become the father of that child.)

Now, DNA in a paternity case is automatic; and the lawyering is gone. Results are either 0% or 99.9999%. The Courts do not have to waste their time litigating such legal intricacies as opportunity, inclination, or intent. He either is or is not the father; the science controls.

But that is now. Then, the science was, if you will pardon the pun, in its infancy.

Unfortunately, I had the client I had. He did not deny the sexual relationship. The HLA results were conclusive.

Instead, what I argued in Court yielded the biggest laugh I

ever received in a Courtroom, which was not the intended result when making a serious legal argument. *"He withdrew."*

Needless to say, you can't win them all.

————

Most of my cases were matters that were referred to me by other lawyers.

Two cases of note were sent to me from a lawyer who had been in my bunk while in summer camp during the 1960s. He was the only non-family member who was a guest both at my own Bar Mitzvah and that of my son. We knew each other well.

He had referred a woman to me because her "sugar daddy" was a client of his firm.

This woman was a stripper by profession who coincidentally worked at a club that employed another one of my clients at the time.

I was to develop a subspecialty representing strippers.

In any event, my friend reviewed the legal issues involved in this prospective case, after which I told him I had only one question.

Thinking I was going to ask some esoteric legal issue, I instead asked my one-word question: *"Implants?"*

There was a long pause, during which I realized that this was not the most professional of questions, before he answered.

I should never have asked the question; and I always wished I could have kept my big mouth shut.

This client ultimately did not hire me, but not because of that.

Before she hired me, she asked me for the referral of a private investigator that she could hire to have her allegedly cheating husband followed and proven to be in *flagrante delicto.*

I referred her to the investigator that I had been using for at least two decades.

Shortly thereafter, when I called to follow up as to whether she would be retaining me, she told me, *"YOUR investigator was made,"* meaning that her husband had spotted the tail. *"There is no way I'm using you as my lawyer!"*

I did not participate in the investigation, but I was held responsible for errors believed to have been made by the one I referred.

Lesson learned. I would never again even suggest an investigator or any other professional without first having been retained by the client.

———

WHILE ON THE SUBJECT of my subspecialty, my other client in that profession told me that she wanted to bring in another of her co-workers who had a non-family law-related legal issue. She brought in her friend, who went on to explain that one of the friend's breast implants had exploded (imploded?). The friend wanted to sue her doctor. I thought that in addition to the doctor, she might also want to sue the manufacturer of the implant itself.

I explained that neither medical malpractice nor product liability were areas to which my law practice extended, but that I would be happy to refer her to an expert in that field.

She really wanted me to be her lawyer and kept trying to get me to reconsider.

We then engaged in the following exchange, which included a stupid and then an extremely smart remark from me:

"I'm looking at you; I don't see any difference."

"That's because I have stuffed that side. Let me show you what I really look like," while starting to take off her top. *"No, no, no! That is not necessary; and I don't think you should do that in my office."*

With the help of her friend/my other client, we convinced her to stay dressed.

She was referred to three different lawyers who handled these personal injury, medical malpractice and product liability cases. I advised each of them to make sure that she did not undress in their offices.

————

THE SAME LAWYER friend who had referred the stripper to me (the one whose husband had "made" my investigator) also referred another potential client to my office.

She was a reporter on a local New York City television station's morning news program. She was married to one of the morning anchors of another local television morning news program.

This woman came to the office with a girlfriend of hers, one of the meteorologists for a third local television station.

I was familiar with the meteorologist as I regularly watched her station, but totally unfamiliar with the potential client.

As we discussed her case, it became apparent that I did not watch her morning news show.

"If you don't watch my channel, what do you watch in the morning?"

Instead of saying something smart, like *"I watch your friend's station,"* I opted for the truth and said, *"Actually, I watch your husband."*

"Home come?"

I was totally flabbergasted and did not know how to respond, and again opted for the truth, telling her that I had "a thing" for his female co-anchor. Perhaps, *"I don't watch TV in the morning"* would have been a better response.

This potential client would never be heard from again.

CHAPTER 14
NOT STUPID, BUT...

A MAN CAME to me for a divorce from his wife.

She countersued him for domestic violence claiming that he was physically abusive of him.

He said/she said. Right?

Nevertheless, I did not like my guy's chances on the domestic violence claim.

Thankfully, we had an inexperienced lawyer on the other side without the wherewithal to object to irrelevant questioning as well as a Judge who was willing to hear any kind of evidence presented and who was not going to rule on objectionable matters without objection from the lawyer.

Even more thankfully, we were in the infancy of the internet; and he had a wife who was interested in getting on with the rest of her life.

She chose to list herself on sugardaddy.com as she looked for a rich new boyfriend or potential husband.

My client referred me to this site where his wife was listed and where photographs of her in various stages of undress were prominently displayed.

I used this fact for all it was worth, claiming that the alleged domestic violence was manufactured by a woman who simply wanted out of her marriage and was actively looking for a new man to take care of her.

The trial was several hours over a single day.

During my cross-examination of the wife, I must have used the term *"sugar daddy dot com"* thirty or more times.

Had I been on the other side, I would have been on my feet at each and every utterance of that term, yelling *"Objection! Irrelevant to the issue before the Court."*

My adversary was silent.

Had I been the trial judge, I would not have allowed my use of that term even in the absence of an objection.

The trial Judge said nothing.

At the end of the day, we were successful; and the domestic violence complaint was dismissed "with prejudice," which meant that the issue was finally resolved and that the wife could not again make that argument on those allegations.

My client was ecstatic and wanted to buy me a drink in celebration.

Ordinarily, my response to such an invitation, would have been, *"That's not necessary. You will get my bill."*

This time, however, I told him, *"Sorry, but I feel very dirty about this. I need to go home to take a shower."*

CHAPTER 15
THE DEATH

SOME STORIES ARE JUST TOO absurd to ignore.

After more than 40 years of being a courtroom attorney, I have seen many things and heard even more. Indeed, one of my former adversaries had a massive coronary in the elevator of the New York County Supreme Court building. He was dead before he hit the floor.

In all this time, I have met a lot of lawyers. At the beginning of my practice, they were almost all older than me. As I retire, they are mostly younger than me.

Then there are the contemporaries.

One day in my later years of practice, I was in Court awaiting the arrival of my client.

Across the room, there was a lawyer of roughly my own age whom I had known for at least 30 years, talking with his client.

Not wishing to interrupt a lawyer-client conversation, I sat back and reviewed my notes.

Eventually, this guy walked away from his client and over to me.

"Larry Bloom?" he asked like he was not sure it was me.

"*Yes?*" I questionably answered, calling him by his first name.

"*I thought you were dead.*"

"*I am very much alive. Where did you hear that? Who told you that?*"

He did not answer.

Oh, the strange things that happen in a Courthouse.

CHAPTER 16
THE SEX

ONCE UPON A TIME, many divorce attorneys had sex with their clients. So much so that a New York City politician, trying to make a name for himself, decided that the best way to do so was to create ethical guidelines governing the Matrimonial Bar. The highlight of these guidelines was a prohibition of lawyers "commencing" a sexual relationship with a client.

D'uh. Wasn't that obvious?

And what does "commencing" mean? Apparently, it is not objectionable to *continue* a sexual relationship with a client if the physical relationship started before the lawyer was retained.

Nevertheless, stories in this regard were legion.

Indeed, the one divorce attorney I knew socially before becoming one myself told me the following when learning of my ascent (descent?) into the field: *"It's a great way to make a living. You get laid a lot!"*

And I knew his wife and his daughter! Did he really have to tell me this?

The answer to your obvious question is this: Did I ever violate this guideline? No, I never commenced a sexual relationship with a client.

Not that I wasn't tempted.

———

THE STRIPPER that I represented from the beginning to the end of her divorce (who had brought in her colleague with the imploded implant), was a beautiful woman with whom there was chemistry.

But I always considered her both a client and a friend, as she originally came to me as the childhood friend of my secretary.

As a young family man in a small New Jersey suburb, I had a circle of friends that included the fathers of my daughter's friends.

One of those fathers was celebrating his 40th birthday. The others wanted to celebrate at a strip club.

I suggested the club where this client, as well as others, had been dancing.

Upon my arrival with two carloads of men in their 40s, the management was happy to see me; and this client, called out, "Laahh!" a shortened version of my first name.

When I responded with the shortened version of her first name (unusually, also her stripper name), our typical greetings for each other, she jumped off the stage, ran over to me, and gave me a big hug and kiss.

Watching were the bunch of guys each of whose wives were all friends with my wife.

On the way home (as each of them was too involved else-where to confront me while we were out) and for days and weeks after, I got questions about my "relationship" with this young woman.

I don't think that any one of them thought I was being truthful when I said she was just a client and a friend.

———

I HAD A CLIENT who I can only describe as a Shiksa[4] Goddess. Physically gorgeous and a truly nice, personable human being.

Part of my job has always been as a fashion consultant; I told people what to wear to Court. *"You look too good,"* I told her. *"Limit the make-up and jewelry. Tie your hair back. Dress very conservatively and, for God's sake, no heels."* We had a frumpy female Judge; and I did not want to have this Judge judging my Christie Brinkley-doppelganger of a client (albeit my client was slightly shorter). This client actually listened, and she even brought her heels with her in a brown paper bag so that she would have them when she left the Court House.

I could not understand why she was getting divorced. The reason? Her husband decided to play for the other team.

At one point, she said to me, *"Give me a call when your wife is out of town."*

But I was a good boy and never crossed the line. That doesn't mean that I didn't want to.

Frankly, I don't know if she was serious about this or not. (I remember a girl in high school referencing one of my friends and saying, *"I love his ass!"* I responded by saying to her, *"You never loved my ass."* *"Wanna bet?"* she said in reply. More than fifty years later, I remember it. I doubted the veracity of this comment then; and I continue to do so now.)

Nevertheless, whether the client was pretending or not, I was near the end of my marriage, and her words were an inspiration. Following her remark, I started an exercise regimen and lost a

____

4. "Shiksa" is the Yiddish term for a non-Jewish woman.

good thirty pounds. (After my separation, I would lose even more.)

———

POSSIBLY SURPRISINGLY, "FASHION CONSULTANT" has been a large part of my professional services. I have even given fashion directives to male clients.

I represented a movie star in a baby-daddy custody case against his television star baby-mama (who would later go on to win an Academy Award). They were never married; thus, there was no divorce case. There was also no issue of paternity, as he acknowledged that he was the father years before my involvement. The financial issues had also been resolved. But the custody case was eventful.

Indeed, after I was first retained, my adversary, whom I had known for a few years, greeted me with, "*Welcome. You are his nineteenth lawyer.*" [It's amazing what a lawyer will do in an attempt to get into the head of the adversary.]

I replied, "*I may be the nineteenth, but I am here now and am the one that you have to worry about.*"

While he was still making movies at the time of my representing him, he had a short-lived television show of his own as the lead playing a prosecuting attorney. One day, I said to him, "*We're going to Court next week. Be on time and wear a suit.*"

"*Why do I have to wear a suit?*" he whined.

In a joke that went entirely over his head, I said, "*You're not a lawyer, but you play one on TV.*"

No reaction whatsoever.

Nevertheless, I was able to convince him to wear a sports jacket and tie; and thankfully, he was on time.

Some 90 minutes after the scheduled appearance, keeping everyone, including the Judge, waiting, the baby-mama strolled into Court without any make-up, with her hair tied back, wearing an old-fashioned (not designer) gray sweatshirt and sweatpants.

"Now, I know why you told me to wear a suit," my client whispered.

Apparently, my adversary omitted the fashion advice.[5]

———

WHILE I REMAIN on the subject of wardrobe appropriate and inappropriate for the Courthouse, I must tell you about one man.

Sometimes, people really do not think things through.

I represented a man who spent a great deal of time in the various casinos in Atlantic City. His propensity for gambling was emphasized by my adversary in the divorce action because of his losses, which were transmuted into an argument of marital economic fault by dissipating marital assets.

The allegation that one's client was guilty of wasteful dissipation in and of itself was one of many that a lawyer is compelled to distract attention from to thus minimize its impact. Sometimes that works; sometimes not.

Well, this one guy arrived at the Courthouse wearing a shiny

---

5. This case also presented a very unusual situation. After my first appearance in Court, an Order was issued that proscribed either party from removing the child from the State of New York. Just before the Memorial Day holiday, the mother took the child with her to another State while she was shooting a movie. My client was understandably upset over this turn of events. Because her action was kidnapping across State lines, I contacted the FBI as well as the Police Commissioner in the State Capitol to which the child had been removed. At one point, I had the FBI on one of my home lines, the Police Commissioner himself on my other (remember fax machines? It was on that line), and my client on my cell phone. After finally convincing the "authorities" that an immediate arrest was the appropriate remedy, my client had second thoughts. He told me, "She is the lead in the movie. If she is arrested, the production will be shut down. When word gets out about this, I will never work again." While I was not thrilled that my good work had been for naught, I was only his lawyer – not his agent, not his career adviser, and not him. The choice was his.

silver satin jacket with the name of a casino emblazoned on his back.

When I saw him that morning, I said, *"Take that thing off and fold it inside out! We don't have time for you to go back to your car to put it fully out of sight. Don't let anyone [meaning his wife or her lawyer or, God forbid, the Judge] catch a glimpse of it."*

Had I been counsel for the wife on that case and had seen this fashion faux pas, I would have been salivating for cross-examination. I would have torn this guy apart.

But alas, I was his lawyer and not hers. The only alternative was to "hide the evidence" to avoid as best we could what could well have been a devastating situation that would have obliterated our chances of success on the merits of the case.

I did not and still to this day cannot believe that a smart and successful businessman could be so oblivious to the optics associated with this blatant fashion error. I would never have thought my client would have been so clueless.

———

IRA, too, was a fashion consultant, although I am sure he never used that phrase.

But he wanted to make sure that no client dressed ostentatiously. His big line was, *"I'm the peacock in the Courtroom!"*

———

A LONG TIME AGO, years before I met the woman who would become my wife and then ex-wife, I hung out with a law school friend when my eyes came upon a beautiful brunette. As anyone who knows me, I am and have always been a sucker for a redhead, with the occasional blonde thrown in. Brunettes were a rarity for me. Well, my friend who had previously dated her caught me watching her and said, *"I know her. Would you like to meet her professionally or personally?"*

I chose the latter.

Watch out for newly separated women!

She was great. Attractive, intelligent, and not too full of herself.

We went out to dinner and then back to her place. I can still remember the taste of her fruit-flavored lipstick. Things went well; and as I left her home, I was looking forward to a second date.

And then I went out to my car to go home.

In those days, cars had aerials, outside metal antennas that stuck up from the hood of the car.

That night, my aerial was broken in half, with the top portion barely attached to the bottom. The (soon-to-be?) ex-husband had been stalking his wife.

I wondered that if the broken antenna was the result of a couple of hours with his wife, what would he attack if I were to spend the entire night with her?

I chose to forego a second date.

Perhaps the better option would have been to have met her as a potential client.

———

ON ANOTHER OCCASION, I represented the wife of a professional athlete; and she was famous in her own right. Probably the most beautiful woman I have ever personally met. We bonded over how stupid her husband was (when his misbehavior was not impacting their child which was truly troublesome and represented a major issue in the custody aspects of her case).

We laughed; we smiled; we flirted. We had chemistry. To say the least, impure thoughts did cross my mind. I am not a saint;

far from it. But something told me, even before the "don't have sex with a client" rule went into effect, that "the next step" would change my life forever; and not in a good way.

I thought that my wife would find out; and that would end my marriage (which happened some twenty years later, albeit for different reasons). It would have thus drastically altered my relationship with my two young children. It would have also changed the nature of my professional relationship with the client as she would then never know if my advice was in her best interests or mine.

As I said, the people were famous. As noted, the husband was a professional athlete with a local team. Before I was on the case, I considered myself to be "a fan." I was also aware that the husband's girlfriend was a well-known actress.

But what I did not know then, only to find out later, was that my client also had a boyfriend and that he was a notorious member of an organized crime family.

My discretion was not merely the better part of valor, but it probably literally saved my life.

———

ON ONE OCCASION, a female client came into the office with a large box filled with sexual paraphernalia. *"This is my husband's porno box."*

"Shemale" videos, books, articles, and women's panties were in the box. Plus, there was an item which I can only describe as the penis enlarger that I had seen in an Austin Powers movie.

Why she gave me this was beyond me; and I told her in several different ways that I did not want the box in my office. I only kept them as possible evidence of the husband's sexual proclivities in the event that a trial might become necessary.

Even when the case was over, the client refused to take her

box back. Into storage, it went for the required seven years of file retention, and then when the time in which a lawyer must retain his old "file," it was junked.

Before you ask, no, I did not watch the videos; nor did I utilize the equipment.

————

DURING THE TIME that I left Ira's employ and my return thereto, while I was with another law firm in a small office building in Suffolk County, I was working on an appeal for a young mother.

As often happened with appellate work, the filing deadline approached a little more quickly than planned. In fact, the client and I were working on the appellate brief all day Thursday before a Friday deadline.

The afternoon wore on into the night. We missed our window for an appellate printer to print, bind, serve, and file the brief in a timely manner. The client and I were working side-by-side, copying and assembling the requisite copies of the brief, and then bound each copy individually to be ready for filing by close of business that Friday in the Appellate Courthouse located in Brooklyn.

Finally, at about 2:00 a.m., we had completed our work and were ready to head to our respective cars for our trips to our homes. We locked the office door and headed downstairs.

Only upon arriving at the door of the building did we realize that the building was locked and that we had no way of getting out through any of the entrances/exits used during the day. I had spent years working for Ira in a Manhattan office tower, a 24-hour building with a night security guard manning the front desk. Not being able to leave the building at night had never been a consideration before and had not then occurred to me.

We returned upstairs to the office whereupon I directed the

young woman to the couch in the boss's private office while I went to my own office to catch a nap before the beginning of the business day on Friday. Early the next morning, with the front door to the building being unlocked, the client drove herself home while I went to Brooklyn to meet the filing deadline.

She had not touched me that night; nor I her.

This fact was irrelevant to the secretaries and other lawyers with whom I was then working. For the next week or two, they bombarded me with a sarcastic, *"Sure, you didn't."*

———

So why a chapter on sex?

The most common question I am asked is, *"What is the number one reason for divorce?"* I love this question. It lets me answer with this three-letter word: *"SEX."*

"No, c'mon. Really. What causes divorces?"

I always repeat, *"It's sex! It could be too much, too little, too straight, too kinky, too boring, someone else, or switching teams."*

"That can't be the reason."

At this point during these conversations, I usually concede that it isn't entirely true that sex is the major cause of divorce. It is communication; it is about yelling and screaming, not listening or even hearing, and sometimes it is about not even speaking with each other. *"Besides,"* I tell them, *"if you are communicating with your spouse, you are having good sex."*

———

Over the years, the second most often asked questions are *"Do you represent more women or men?"* and then, *"Do you prefer to represent women or men?"*

Over the course of more than 40 years of professional practice,

I would have to say that it has probably been 50-50; but it has been streaky depending on my stage of life, the manner in which I obtained clients, and the luck of the draw.

As for my preference, which was usually the follow-up question, my standard line has been: *"Men are better payers, women are better stories."*

———

OF ALL OF THE STORIES, hands down, my favorite is this: Throughout my practice, and particularly before the no-fault grounds for divorce were enacted, I always had my clients write down for me, preferably in their own handwriting, their reasons for getting divorced. I did this for two reasons: 1) I needed to know the background for the initial papers in the case, be it a complaint for divorce or a motion to the Court seeking interim relief (usually something to do with money or the children); and 2) I wanted to make sure that I could never be accused of making anything up.

One woman gave me her story that was graphic, to say the least. Her husband wanted her (his wife) and another woman in bed together with him; he wanted a menage-a-trois. In order to get her there, he worked her up by encouraging and engaging in various forms of group sex. I am certainly not a prude; but some of the combinations she detailed for me were beyond my prior comprehension and certainly beyond my imagination (at least to that point).

Without giving all of the facts that still make me blush, I remind the reader of Murphy's Law: *Whatever can go wrong, will go wrong.*

Needless to say, my client's husband had his prayers answered. He brought another woman into the marital bed. The problem for him was that my client liked it so much that she realized that she preferred the new woman to her husband, and that his part of the sexual relationship was superfluous. (And that was what brought her into my office in the first place.)

My problem when I reviewed her X-rated diary was one of distraction. Every time I tried to read through the entire explicit dissertation, the phone would ring or a client would come in to see me or something else diverted my attention. The only viable option I had was to bring this thing home to give it the attention it deserved without interruption outside of normal working hours.

Murphy's Law continued for me.

Like a complete idiot, I left the document home one day.

This resulted in my getting a phone call from the missus. *"What is this pornography? How can you leave this just lying around the house?"* I explained that I routinely had clients write their "story" as well as the reasons for it. I then told her about being interrupted in the office.

When she finally calmed down, she asked, *"What does she look like?"*

I could not help myself and responded, *"A lot better after reading this!"*

Not a good answer.

———

THIS WAS ALSO about the same time I was representing the "Lee sisters." A guy I knew from law school was representing two of the husbands of three of my clients who were sisters; and he mentioned "the Lee sisters" to me.

I had no idea what he was talking about until he said, "Home, Ug and Ghast." I do not want any of my readers to think that all of my clients were gorgeous; "the Lee sisters" was an apt description.

———

ANOTHER COMMON QUESTION that I get concerns whether I ever attempted to match-make with my clients.[6]

I tried match-making once. That was enough.

How do you set up clients? Simple.

At that time, I made appointments for both clients at the same time; I had hoped that the magic might happen.

On this occasion, I really thought the male and female clients would be a good fit. They share an age group with similarly aged children; they were of the same ethnicity; and they were both attractive albeit vertically challenged.

I told neither client in advance of their "appointments" (which also were for me to discuss a minor matter with each of them), but I was compelled to mention it to him when she was late for the scheduled meeting, and we had concluded his business for the day. I needed to say something to get him to stay in the office. He was intrigued. I never said anything to her.

Well, she flew into the office clearly upset about her case, ranting and raving, far worse than I had experienced from her even with her Type A personality. She blew in; she erupted; she blew out.

He: *"You wanted me to go out with THAT?!?"*

Never again did I attempt to put two people together.

As I have often said to clients who truly did not want to be divorced, as well as to acquaintances asking about "setups," *I am in the business of breaking 'em up, not putting 'em together.*

———

———

6. 1. I get this almost as much as my father's question often repeated by others, "Do your clients ever reconcile?" My answer to that was always, "Don't use that vile language with me! We never mention the 'R' word!"

THERE WAS ANOTHER CLIENT who had been referred to me by our mutual accountant.

She was a dead ringer for a very famous model with whom she shared her accent. She was a sweetheart who could not have been a nicer person. If possible, she was even more beautiful on the inside than she was on the outside.

There were moments both during and after our lawyer-client relationship where the line could have been crossed. I do not believe either of us would have protested an advance by the other at any time during or after the legal representation.

For whatever reason, we kept our relationship professional and have remained friends for more than a decade after the lawyer-client relationship concluded.

———

OF COURSE, this chapter would not be complete without mentioning the unfounded and unbased allegations made by clients accusing me of wanting to drop the fee in exchange for sex. This happened on more than one occasion.

One client even went so far as to say this to a woman lawyer with whom I shared office space. God bless her; my colleague said to my client, *"Everyone knows Larry Bloom wouldn't stick his dick into anything that owed him money!"*.

A little unrefined, but it did make me feel better as my worries dissolved into laughter.

It was also as true a statement about me as I have ever heard.

CHAPTER 17
THE LOVE

THERE IS A TELEVISION AD prevalent in South Florida for a personal injury law firm. Their tagline, and what you hear various clients repeat throughout this repetitive series of their ads is: *"I love my attorneys!"*

Divorce attorneys do not hear much of this.

We are more likely to hear, *"I hate my divorce lawyer"* or, even more often, *"I hate my wife's [or husband's] divorce lawyer."*

But once I felt the love, however misplaced it may have been.

———

I HAD REPRESENTED a woman throughout her divorce, which took well over a year.

The case was not unusual. It was a short-term, childless marriage. My client was a 30-something woman from Eastern Europe. Other than her accent, she was not remarkable – not tall and not short, not fat and not skinny, and not pretty or ugly.

After the case was over and she had her final divorce papers, she asked for an appointment.

On the day of our appointment, my twenty-something-year-old daughter was working the front reception desk while my secretary took the day off.

When the client, who had dressed herself up with makeup and hair done like she had never done before, walked in, she closed the door to my private office (something I never did when I was meeting alone with a female client), before announcing, *"Mr. Bloom [NOT Larry], I'm in love with you."*

"No, you're not."

"Yes, I am."

"No, you are not!"

"Really, I'm in love with you."

"I'm your lawyer. Trust me."

"What are you talking about?"

"You have Florence Nightingale Syndrome. I was there when you needed someone to listen to you and to address your needs. I did those things. I took care of you. You are thankful. You are appreciative. But you are not in love with me!"

"Are you sure?"

"I am very sure."

CHAPTER 18
THE FEAR

I HAVE NEVER BEEN afraid of bullies.

But there was a single occasion when I truly feared for my life.

It was not the time that I represented the wife of a professional athlete. I was not afraid of him or of my client's *Mafioso* boyfriend. Perhaps, I should have been, but I was not.

My past representations included clients who were "connected," or clients of the "connected's" wives or girlfriends. Never had there been any problem. But on one occasion, I represented a man who was slight in stature. He was an Israeli with a strong accept. He was a little excitable, even in the initial interview; but both with divorce clients and Israelis, that was not unusual.

Perhaps the fact that he had a "carry permit," a license to carry a loaded firearm, should have been an indication of trouble. But there was an explanation for his carrying a loaded gun with him everywhere he went. He was in the vending machine business and held large amounts of cash at all hours of the day and night. If he qualified to "carry" under the laws of New York and

New Jersey (two of the most difficult jurisdictions in which to obtain such a permit), I did not then question my own safety.[7]

Indeed, if you had met him when I did – the same day that he hired me as his lawyer – you would have found him to be no one out of the ordinary other than having an obvious hatred for his wife – which for a divorce litigant is par for the course.

But that first day, when he interviewed with me and retained me (usually at least a two-meeting process, sometimes more), was the only time I ever saw him not hopped up on crack.

Each time I saw him, he became more and more agitated. He had a hair-trigger anger that erupted with the slightest provocation – sometimes, without any justification whatsoever.

During divorce negotiations, there are often four-way meetings. Each spouse is present, as are their respective attorneys. Hence, the name "four-way."

However, when I had a "four-way" scheduled to take place at the offices of his wife's lawyer, the meeting became a "six-way." There were three separate lawyers in the firm at this meeting along with their client to negotiate with me and my client.

This prompted jokes from me about them needing three lawyers to negotiate against me; and it also prompted me to make very clear that any future motion for legal fees on behalf of the wife would be met by this manifest padding of their bills. In fact, after the meeting, I memorialized this comment in writing to make sure that I had a writing to counter any future application for fees.

While the lawyers were undoubtedly each billed to the wife, the presence at the meeting of three strong men was likely because the wife was scared to death of her husband.

---

7. When I tried to get a carry permit for my cousin, I told him it would never be granted because there were strict requirements for such a permit. He insisted that I seek the permit anyway, I filed the necessary paperwork and tried my best to get within the guidelines necessary, only to have his application denied.

Although he was on his best behavior at this settlement conference, he continued to grow increasingly angry with me.

The longer the litigation went on without resolution, the more threatening he became.

I admit it. I was terrified.

Finally, I had to advise this client to obtain new counsel and that his failure to do so would be met with an application to the Court to be removed as his lawyer, wherein I would detail my fear and the basis for it.

He got another lawyer.

CHAPTER 19
THE ISSUES

ONE WOULD THINK that divorce law was the same thing over and over again. After all, it is just 'get them divorced, split their property, split the kids, and provide support.'

Or is it?

While sometimes the facts are repetitive, the variations are unique – and not just the salacious ones.

The legal issues can be complex.

On one particular occasion, a man came to see me about an appeal. He was found to have abused his child. These are not the types of cases I enjoy addressing, but they are certainly not isolated.

Upon questioning him further – and then later reading the lower Court record – I discovered that he had not done anything. I am not saying this as an advocate. He did not do *anything*!

But there was something that made his case unusual.

This gentleman was trying to quit smoking; and he had a dream that he harmed his child. He related this dream to his psychotherapist in a session; and the therapist considered herself obligated, as a mandatory reporting health care professional, to advise the child welfare agency about a perceived danger to the child. Whether or not my client had his own cause of action against the therapist was the subject of discussions that I had with him; but when he realized that he would need another lawyer to do this, he rejected the idea.

My client admitted his dream in Court and brought in an expert to testify about nicotine withdrawal, which included vivid dreams and nightmares for the person going through the withdrawal. The trial Judge apparently did not care and issued a finding of abuse against my client. I am sure the Judge did not want his name in the paper if, at a later date, my client did, in fact, harm his child.

Not a single allegation, let alone a shred of evidence, existed about my client actually harming or even threatening to harm his child.

My arguments concerning the lack of any real threat and about my client's withdrawal from nicotine addiction carried the day.

The media (at least *The New York Post*) deemed this novelty in the law and brought me my first "ink" – the first time my name appeared in a newspaper. It would not be the last.

————

THEN, there was the man who came into the office with a very unusual yet delicate issue.

First of all, this was a man who was a doppelganger for the nerdy newsman on the old television show, *WKRP in Cincinnati*. His physical appearance, along with the fact that he was a practicing attorney himself, made the situation all the more striking.

His issue? He was a bigamist. He married for a second time without bothering to divorce wife #1.

Unfortunately, bigamy is deemed to be a "crime of moral

turpitude." Were his situation to be made public, the man could well have lost his livelihood, as the commission of a crime of moral turpitude is a ground for disbarment.

One would think that a successful lawyer would have realized the potential disaster of marrying a second woman before ending the marriage with the first.

Yet, the heart wants what the heart wants.

The potential client had come in with a woman, wife #1, who went on to tell me that this nebbish-looking man was a sex addict. It was not just a matter of what the heart wanted, but rather a lower portion of his anatomy.

After she gave me the facts – which her husband, my client, was not inclined to disclose – I asked her to leave the room. I did this for a variety of reasons. In particular, I made clear that there were attorney-client privilege issues that might be jeopardized if my client were to make statements in the presence of a non-lawyer.

But the reasons that I wanted to speak with the client alone were two-fold (and I knew better than to expect a truthful answer while she was present):

1. Did he want to remain married to either of them?

2. If so, which one did he want to keep?

I also told him that were he to die with two "wives," all hell would break loose in terms of his estate. There was no question that he had to do *something* to protect himself.

I also explained that the course of action depended on his answers.

The second marriage, the one to wife #2, although bigamous under the eyes of the law, was also not valid under those same eyes. Simply stated, a person cannot have more than one spouse at a time.

Whichever wife he wanted to keep, the second marriage had to be legally declared to be a void marriage; he could not simply divorce #2. Even if he wanted to stay married to wife #2, he had to bring on an action to declare the nullity of this marriage considered under the eyes of the law to be "void." In addition to that, he also had to legally divorce wife #1. However, if he were not careful, wife #1, also known as the woman spurned, could have made the man's life a living hell by publicizing the bigamy. On the flip side, were wife #1 to go public, she would be jeopardizing her own support since she would have killed the proverbial golden goose by removing the husband's ability to earn a living. Consequently, the prudent path was to declare the second marriage void before divorcing the first. Only when both marriages were terminated (one declared void and the other divorced) could the man legally marry wife #2.

Fortunately, he wanted to keep wife #1 which simplified things significantly, as we only had to declare the nullity of the void second marriage. But it was only simple in the fact that there was only one lawsuit to be filed.

That remaining lawsuit was not as simple as it sounds. Even though the man was never legally married to wife #2, he was still on the hook for spousal support and for a property distribution of the assets acquired during the "marriage." Whatever property that was acquired between the time he said "I do" for the second time to the time he brought on formal proceedings to declare the marriage void was still subject to an equitable distribution by the Court as it was technically "marital property" under the definition of that term in the statute regardless of the void nature of the "marriage."

In other words, my guy had some very serious problems.

We sued to declare the nullity of the void second marriage.

When wife #2 hired a lawyer, there were even more concerns.

The lawyer she selected was one I had only known in passing, but whose reputation as a fighting litigator had preceded him.[8]

But this lawyer also was no fool. Risking my client's disbarment was not going to be beneficial to his client as the end of my client's livelihood through disbarment would have killed the golden goose in terms of money that was available to pay her spousal maintenance.

My fighting for every penny for my guy was also too risky.

Without any leverage on my part, we made a generous settlement offer, which, after negotiations, was tweaked higher. No one wanted to kill the golden goose. The marriage was declared legally void without the Court ever being apprised of the career of my client… and they all lived happily ever after.

———

EARLY IN MY LEGAL CAREER, in the early 1980s, near the time when I started working for Ira Bennett, we had another potentially bigamous situation.

While we did not have a lawyer involved who risked disbarment, we did have another complication of common-law marriage.

Our client, the husband, was an older gentleman who owned one of the more well-known restaurants in Manhattan.

His wife of more than forty years was divorcing him for several different reasons, including the fact that he had a long-term girlfriend.

That girlfriend, I learned, had been around since well before the marriage.

---

8. A few years after this case was resolved, the man had a massive coronary in the Courthouse elevator and was dead before it reached the first floor.

Indeed, this woman had been his girlfriend since the early 1930s.

Common law marriage – marriage without the benefit of a marriage license or ceremony – had once been legal in New York, as it had once been legal in the other 49 States. It was not until 1933 that New York discontinued recognizing common-law marriages.

An argument could well have been made that my client was not legally married to his wife since he had been lawfully common law married to the girlfriend at the time of the later marriage. In such a case, my client would not merely have had a substantial liability to the wife but also to the girlfriend, who, fortunately, never considered herself anything more than his girlfriend.

I raised the issue with Ira; he wisely told me to ignore it.

We were able to resolve the divorce without the necessity of addressing the legality of a common-law marriage to either the wife or the girlfriend. But I did have some sleepless nights.

———

ONE DAY, I arrived back at the office following Court when my secretary told me that she had received a call from a woman with a name that was not unknown to me and that an appointment had been made for an initial consultation.

I asked my secretary if this was the same woman as in the case bearing that name. A case entitled that name against that same name was the then leading case in the State of New York from a then-recent ruling of the First Department of the Appellate Division for cases arising out of Manhattan and the Bronx. This case stood for the principle that where there is a large disparity in the financial abilities of the two parties to a divorce suit, the Court is not merely entitled to award the needier spouse (usually the wife) a substantial legal fee to that party's attorney, but is in fact obligated to do so.

My secretary had not asked, but following the consultation, I told her that the prospective client was indeed the one of caselaw fame.

I was then retained as her second lawyer. (It is extremely rare for the first lawyer in a hotly contested divorce case to be the last lawyer; lawyers are routinely replaced.)

What a case! It was truly the case of a lifetime and resulted in the largest fee I ever earned on a single case in my illustrious career.

The facts of the case were these:

The husband and the wife were both Swiss Nationals where they had married and had four young children. The wife had been a pediatrician in Switzerland; the husband was, as he later testified on trial, "an international attorney and businessman."

I had the case for two years, seven weeks of trial as well as the second appeal on the case. I never really knew what he did for a living, but I had my suspicions. Why seven weeks? The trial extended partially because even though everyone in the Courtroom spoke English fluently and had some passing knowledge of French (with each party being fluent in French), the husband insisted upon testifying in his native language of French. The first day of the trial was a complete waste of time because the public (cost-free) interpreter provided by the Courts was painfully weak in translation, leading to the retention of a private interpreter paid by the husband.[9]

The parties also had a prenuptial agreement; and the only substantive issues were the children, spousal and child support, and legal fees. The prenup had resolved all property issues.

The married couple had decided to "sojourn" (their word) in New York with the children for a year. The mother took a sabbatical from medicine. The children were enrolled in a French-speaking private school in Manhattan. The father traveled back and forth between New York and Switzerland, as well as to many other places around the globe, including several trips to the Middle East.

Before I came aboard, each party had initially had his/her own lawyer, with the husband having already substituted out the

---

9. Several years later, I represented a working-class man who had immigrated from Italy. He was financially successful and acquired various assets in the form of real estate holdings. During the divorce action, the wife's lawyer wanted to depose my client. (A deposition is a formal questioning of someone under oath during the discovery portion of litigation to obtain disclosure of facts that is utilized to prepare for trial; and the best preparation leads to leverage used in settlement negotiations to obtain an optimal resolution for the client.). The other lawyer in that matter arranged for both a court stenographer and an interpreter as my client truly needed to testify in Italian. While a free inter-preter is available in Court, a private interpreter needed to be employed for a deposition; and since the adversary needed to obtain the discovery, he and hisclient were obligated to select the individual interpreter and to pay for this service. During the formal questioning of my client which took place in the office of the wife's lawyer, the interpreter that my adversary had employed was unable to translate the word "mortgage." Indeed, by the third attempt at translation, it was painfully apparent that this interpreter would never find an adequate translation of the word into Italian. Having a client to represent, and with the court stenographer taking down every English word used by the parties and the lawyers, I made a full record relative to the inability of the interpreter to properly perform her job before announcing that "this deposition is over" and then walking out of the office with my client. The adversary could not very well challenge any refusal to provide discovery without making public his own incompetence in hiring an unqualified interpreter.

first firm to represent him. I became the second attorney for the wife. There had been motion practice involving temporary support, access to the children and fees. The Court's denial of a temporary (*"pendente lite"*) counsel fee led to the first appeal, which was decided before my involvement.

That first appeal in this matter determined a Statewide standard that an award of counsel fees should not be denied at the outset of the litigation, particularly where, as in this case, one party had a gross disparity of the assets and earnings power.

In subsequent years, this issue would be heard in various other matters before the Court of Appeals in Albany, the highest Court of the State of New York. Those other determinations from the highest Court with State-wide applicability have since taken over as the standard established by this case which had been issued by one of the four Judicial Departments of the State.

When I came in, I was also awarded a fee, before the same trial-level Judge to whom this matter had been assigned. (There is a general rule for all cases, not just divorces, that for one case, there is only one Judge per case. Only if there is a reason for the Judge's recusal, he or she dies, retires, or is reassigned, will there ever be a new Judge assigned to a case.) After the trial, I was awarded yet another substantial legal fee paid by the husband.

I was provided with the file from the outgoing counsel for the wife. It was more than forty boxes worth of papers, the review of which was a cumbersome task. But what a treasure trove!

This particular matter was about preparation. I painstakingly reviewed everything in these more than forty boxes. Every case involves preparation. Indeed, the general rule of thumb is that a lawyer devotes two hours of preparation to every hour spent in Court. This case was so paper-laden as to exponentially increase the time I devoted to readying this matter for trial.

But that preparation led to incredible results, providing me with the ammunition for my cross-examination of the husband.

There was quite a bit to cross-examine him about, which added to the length of the trial.

Included were all of the husband's Swiss bank records that had carefully been redacted to exclude all names to comply with Swiss banking laws (always referred to by the husband and his lawyers as the "Swiss Secrecy Laws") and to help the husband hide as much information as possible. But the numbers reflecting transactions, deposits, and withdrawals, were telling; there were seven- and eight-figure deposits showing up to tens of millions of Euros at a time.

Astounded by the tens of millions of dollars/Euros that went through this Swiss account on a regular basis, I said to my client, *"This is too much to be drug money. It has to be guns!"*

She did not respond, leading me to believe that my conclusion had merit. Unfortunately, despite my very strong suspicions, I had no proof that the husband was an arms dealer. As my client was not inclined to address the topic, and for other reasons, I dropped the topic and did not pursue it further either in discovery or at trial. Those other reasons included the potential disclosure before the Court of the criminal activity of the husband, which the Judge would have been duty-bound to refer to the appropriate law enforcement authorities – which could very well have jeopardized the husband's ability to provide spousal support and child support – I did not want to kill this golden goose. I did not act further on my suspicions.

Nevertheless, this flow of tens of millions going through the husband's Swiss bank account monthly also put into question the veracity of the husband's testimony as well as the veracity of his United States income tax returns showing an income of only $160,000 per year.

Also included in the multitude of papers provided was an application for a rental apartment that the husband leased after the separation of the parties. Immediately before his signature were the typed words to the effect that he was submitting his application "under penalty of perjury" as to the truth of his representations.

In that financial statement made "under penalty of perjury," he set forth an annual income of $502,000. It was not an admission of the millions in annual income that I believed existed but nevertheless a lie of substance.

This led to the question that every trial lawyer dreams of being able to ask on cross-examination, *"You just testified to earning $160,000; and you filed tax returns showing that income. And here you submit under penalty of perjury that your income is over half a million dollars annually. ARE YOU LYING NOW OR WERE YOU LYING THEN? OR ARE YOU LYING WITH BOTH OF THESE REPRESENTATIONS?"*

This is the proverbial smoking gun.

We continued on this trial that lasted seven weeks, trying it two weeks at a time with a few weeks between each such trial period.

I continued in cross-examination of the husband while being ready to ask further questions to prove he paid his second lawyer $1 Million.

"How much did you pay your first lawyer, Ms. E?"

"About $400,000," the husband replied.

"And how much did you pay your current counsel, Mr. S?"

"$2.1 Million."

I quickly flipped over my next ten pages of notes to move on to another topic.[10] My questioning him about the fees had become unnecessary with this admission.

The trial continued to a conclusion since neither party was

---

10. I have often been told by judges that when you have made your point, move on; when you are winning, be quiet. It is advice that I regularly give friends in situations that have nothing to do with the law: when you are winning, shut up!

ready to compromise on where the children would reside. The Judge ultimately rendered a trial decision. It was a ruling that made neither party happy, as is often the case with trials.

The Judge granted my client custody of the children; and she directed the husband to pay substantial child support plus all extras, including private school and college. I was awarded another very substantial fee to be paid by the husband. (My argument that I should be compensated to the same degree as the husband paid his own lawyer – over $2 Million – fell on deaf ears.)

However, my client was unhappy due to both the amount of spousal support and the one-year duration of such maintenance. The Judge was unmoved by my client's desire to be a music therapist, earning $25,000 per year when she could have easily practiced medicine and earned ten times that amount.

The husband, too, believed he had lost because the Judge refused to direct the return of the children from New York to Switzerland.

Fast forward two years. There is a call of motions before the same Judge on her regular matrimonial calendar before a Courtroom overflowing with lawyers. I am in the room, as is Mr. S, trial counsel for the husband in the Swiss case, each of us present on unrelated and differing matters.

The Judge was addressing two young lawyers (and by then I had apparently graduated to a middle-aged lawyer) arguing an issue of counsel fees. The Judge interrupted the argument, saying, *"I'm going to second call this. I see Mr. Bloom in the back of the room. He's the expert on counsel fees. Go talk to him."*

The youngsters obediently followed the request of the Court (like they had a choice) and approached me in the back of the room.

I said to them, *"While I am well conversant with the law on* *counsel fees, Mr. S over there is the true expert. He made $2.1 Million on the C case; and I earned far less."*

Mr. S shook his head from side to side, indicating a negative response.

I raised my thumb, silently asking him if it was more, to which he responded by shaking his head up and down.

"All right," I asked him, *"How much?"*

"By the time it was over, $2.6 Million."

In other words, the husband paid his two lawyers $3 Million; and he also paid the two lawyers who represented his wife another $500,000 or more!

Was it worth it? Maybe it would have been worth it to him had the Court ruled for the children to be returned to Switzerland as he had sought. But I cannot see any divorce – particularly where there were no property issues – costing that much in legal fees.

———

I REPRESENTED A WIFE in the same County in which I resided just before my own separation from my wife.

The husband was not paying his wife anything in either alimony or child support, let alone the amounts he had been directed to pay by the same Judge.

The case had been assigned to the chief matrimonial Judge in that County.

I had made many appearances before this Presiding Judge on this case (as well as on other matters), but my arguments were falling upon deaf ears. I was having trouble prompting the Judge to assure that my client had sufficient funds to support herself and her children.

Finally, one day I was so frustrated that I set aside my notes prepared for an argument before the Court with all appropriate legal precedent; and I chose to argue from the gut.

"Your Honor," I said, *"Not in a million years would I ever advise a client of this, but I am about to become a matrimonial litigant in this County. And I know that the Presiding Judge is not enforcing her own orders when it comes to support. What do you think I am going to do when I am faced with a support order?"*

The Judge looked at me askance and then thought for a moment before looking at the husband and saying, *"Mr. T, this case is adjourned to 9:00 a.m. tomorrow. I expect you here; bring your toothbrush!"*

The toothbrush remark is Judges' code for *"If you don't bring payment in full, I'm sending you to jail."* It also meant that if he did not show up for Court the next day, a warrant would have been issued for his arrest.

He brought the funds the next morning.

———

I WAS BROUGHT into another case to represent the husband when he had already been in jail for his failure to make a $100,000 property distribution payment that was months past due. The girlfriend had retained me to get him out of jail.

After speaking with opposing counsel and the Court, it was clear that the husband would remain incarcerated until he made payment in full. Had he made good faith payments on a regular basis, he would never have been sent to jail in the first place; he would have been given a payment schedule. His persistent failure to pay anything resulted in this most drastic of remedies, as well as the position that he would not be released until there was payment in full.

I was instructed to appear in Court the next morning, where

the girlfriend met us with $80,000 in cash (green money) and a $20,000 cashier's check.

It was magic! Particularly since only a day before, I had been told that he did not have the money, and I had been paid my fee with the girlfriend's personal check.

We got him released.

———

WHILE I WAS STILL in Ira's employ, we had a client who was a used car dealer.

Simultaneously with her commencement of the divorce action, our client's wife obtained temporary restraining orders barring entry to some twenty safety deposit boxes in about a dozen different banks.

Our client was livid. He explained that he had *"over $400,000 in cash in those boxes."* Needless to say, these monies were not reported as income by him to the State and Federal taxing authorities.

The initial resolution by the Court was to have the boxes remain sealed but have the parties and respective counsel review the contents of those boxes and catalog each box's contents.

There was nowhere near $400,000, but rather only about $20,000 in various small bills, mostly $20 bills.

With the actual amount determined and secured, we were able to resolve the cash-in-the-boxes issue quite quickly, with the money being divided four ways between the parties and each of their attorneys.

———

I HAVE BEEN REFERRED CASES from many different lawyers, one of whom was a friend that I had met several decades earlier when he was the Chief Law Clerk to one of the then-two matrimonial judges in Brooklyn. When I started practicing before the Brooklyn Court (also known as the Kings County Supreme Court), there was a single Judge who was assigned every divorce for that County. Were Brooklyn a separate city, it would have been the fourth most populated city in the United States. The fact that there had been only one or two judges hearing every divorce in Brooklyn was insane; they were incredibly overworked, which resulted in months of delays. Now, years later, there are far more judges assigned to the Matrimonial Part in Kings County.

My friend is an observant Orthodox Jew; and he told me how offended he was by the call he had received from a prospective client.

The man had actually said to him, *"I gotta problem, and I need to get me a Jew lawyer!"*

With such an ethnic slur combined with the New Jersey jurisdiction of the case, there was no way that my friend was ever going to represent this man, but he did not want to have a remunerative case entirely lost. He gave the prospective client my name and number.

My friend also knew that I would not send a client away if there was a way to keep the case. While I can be offended as much as anyone, I never lightly set aside business.

The client called and made an appointment.

The story this man told me was intriguing, presenting the type of novel issue that I just loved to litigate.

At the outset, I must point out that what the Judge on his divorce did to him was neither unfair nor unreasonable. The problems that this man faced were entirely of his own making.

My client was a hairstylist who owned a multi-family apartment building in Crown Heights, Brooklyn, worth at least a million dollars. He ran his own hair salon out of the storefront of that building.

Using his original lawyer, an offer was made for the sale of the building and an equal division of the proceeds. The other side wanted no support or anything concerning the salon. They did not even seek anything from his G.I. Pension that he had through his military service; she wanted no alimony.

It was a good offer which he should have jumped at. I certainly would have advised him to do so had I been his lawyer at the time.

However, he maintained, *"I bought it! I fixed it up! I own it! She's not entitled to an f-ing penny!"*

I spoke with his original attorney who confirmed that he told the client that divorce law did not work that way and that his wife was entitled to an equitable distribution of all assets acquired during the marriage. Original counsel also confirmed that the client, nevertheless, was insistent. He would not agree to give her anything.

That left the client and his first lawyer no choice but to have a trial, which took place in due course. This took place before my involvement in the litigation.

Following testimony, the Court did as was requested by the wife. The Judge directed the sale of the building and the equal division of the proceeds of the sale, but with the sum of $5,000 being deducted from the husband's share as his contribution towards his wife's legal fees. The building was worth over a million dollars, with no outstanding mortgage obligation.

Most importantly, the Court also directed that the husband, in whose sole name title to the building was held, not transfer the title out of his name before the formal sale to a *bona fide* purchaser.

The divorce case was in New Jersey, where the wife resided after separating from her husband. The building was in Brooklyn, where the husband resided.

When the case got to me, you guessed it, the husband had

transferred title in direct contravention to the specific Order of the Judge. The New York City Registrar's Office where the real estate records were located confirmed that the husband transferred the million-dollar building to a corporation in the business name of the hair salon for $15,000. A very short time later, that corporation then transferred the building to another corporation nominally having no relation to the husband for $25,000.

I was fairly confident that no money had ever changed hands except for payment to those individuals who had conceived of this scheme on behalf of my client.

Later, during the tenure of my representation of this man, I had the opportunity to visit the officially listed "corporate offices" of this second corporation in whose name the property was ultimately owned. From the people with whom I was able to speak at the "corporate address," there was no record of such an entity ever being at that address. Indeed, no one there had ever heard of it; not had anyone heard of the name of the hair salon nor heard of my client's name. That "corporate address" was, in fact, a residential apartment building with no business of any type operating there.

I was only retained when the wife's lawyers discovered the fraudulent transfers and sought relief against the husband in the form of his incarceration. This was to be the first step in their plan to receive the money awarded to the wife at trial.

So, what was so intriguing? Why take the case at all? After all, what kind of defense did he have? Did he have any defense whatsoever?

Well, this client had a Trustee who was appointed through the Veteran's Association. After speaking with the Trustee who had been assigned to manage the financial affairs of the client including the payment of the mortgage and taxes on the building in question, I learned quite a lot about my client.

The Trustee advised me that my new client had suffered from

PTSD (Post-Traumatic Stress Disorder) after he had fallen out of a helicopter during his military basic training several decades before.

I had a client whose disability had been established by the United States Government. He was so disabled, the Federal Government had determined, as to warrant that a Trustee be appointed to manage at least some of his financial affairs. I was provided with a copy of the disability records, including his detailed psychiatric file; he was a mess. In other words: *He was crazy; and now I had the papers to prove it!* He was not an attractive witness, but one who could be shown to be as crazy as had already been established by the Federal Government.

That Psychiatric Report became Exhibit "A" to my submissions to Courts in both New Jersey and New York since we were compelled to not only fight the contempt motion in New Jersey but also to seek to set aside the New Jersey trial decision; and we also had to respond to the separate lawsuit that would shortly be brought against my client and the various corporate entities in the Courts in Brooklyn, New York, seeking to invalidate the two deeds.

Under United States constitutional law, there is a principle known as "the Federal Supremacy Doctrine," which essentially means that a State authority cannot undermine a determination by the Federal Government.

My guy, who had a federally appointed Trustee, was permitted to go to trial without the involvement of the Trustee and also without a *Guardian Ad Litem* (a law guardian) that should have been, appointed, I argued, because of the inability of the client to act in his own best interests.

Indeed, I would argue, that his alleged violations of the Order to not transfer the property was further evidence of his lack of competence to manage his own affairs as well as his lack of competence to proceed to trial in the New Jersey divorce case.

I took on the case; and I brought on a motion before the same trial Judge to vacate everything (except the divorce itself) because my client was incompetent. I argued that the financial terms of the divorce judgment should be vacated as well as the direction that he was not to transfer the property in Brooklyn.

I provided everyone with notice including the corporate transferees and the Trustee that had previously been appointed for my client by the Veterans' Administration.

My papers were voluminous as they contained the full psychiatric evaluation and the proofs I obtained as to the transfers.

The trial Judge, who had devoted considerable time to the trial as well as pretrial and post-judgment matters, ruled, *"Yeah, He's crazy, all right. Crazy like a fox. He knew exactly what he was doing. He knew what I told him to do and what I told him not to do. Despite that, he violated MY Orders! He is going to jail; and he is going to stay there until he undoes what he did in violation of MY Orders!"*

My client was arrested and taken into custody. He remained incarcerated in the County detention center for the next several months throughout the remainder of my involvement in the matter.

In truth, he and whoever was advising him at the time of the transfers had so confused the title to the property that it was impossible for him to do anything to allow the wife and her attorneys (who were granted authority to arrange for a sale at fair market value) to gain title that was insurable by a title insurance company. Even were he amenable to correcting the error to gain his release, his unlawful actions concerning the two transfers of the property made the desired correction impossible short of a new New York lawsuit specifically seeking the overture of both deeds.

In any event, the client was not inclined to cooperate.

After the incarceration, the wife retained New York counsel to set aside the two transfers and to obtain "clean," insurable title to the property. This was exactly the type of lawsuit that I had suggested to my client to get his release from jail, which my client had already adamantly rejected.

I had no intention of abandoning this matter while my client was incarcerated. But his animosity and venom turned against me – he Blamed Bloom – with the various threats, leaving me no choice but to seek to be removed as his attorney. He had written to me, threatening me both personally and professionally. That letter became the first exhibit in my applications in both States for leave to withdraw as his attorney.

Each Court had no choice but to grant me the relief sought.

———

THE SAME FRIEND who had referred the aforementioned crazy title case, also referred to me a woman who had a divorce case pending in a County in New York State abutting the County in New Jersey where I resided. The Courthouse was a short distance from my home. The case was too far away from his home; and he did not want it.

She was an Orthodox Jew, as was the referring counsel. I was not. I did not wear a yarmulke.

She wanted him. She did not want me.

Nevertheless, she agreed to meet me to discuss her case.

It turned out that her husband had punched her in the stomach during the course of her pregnancy. (She was still pregnant at the time of our consultation.)

I also realized that she had been employed by one of the local Bar Associations and that I had had a passing acquaintance with her. Still, she wanted the Orthodox attorney, and that was definitely not me. She made clear that I was not going to represent her under any circumstance.

I learned further that she had been discharged from her

employment because of the time she necessarily had to take off related to her pregnancy and the injuries sustained from her husband's assault.

"I got it," I told her, *"you would prefer not to have me as your lawyer. I am not everyone's cup of tea. But the truth is, you need two lawyers. You need an employment lawyer because your termination by the Bar Association was unlawful. I am sure that they don't want the publicity surrounding wrongful termination under these circumstances and are likely to settle. Whether or not you hire me for the divorce and other claims against your husband, which may also include an award of damages for the personal injuries you sustained from his attack, I do not do employment law. I would be happy to locate counsel for you in that regard; and I would even be happy to work with such expert counsel if you and such counsel find it appropriate. I understand that you may not want me to represent me in the divorce; and even if you change your mind, I am going to suggest another lawyer to you. She is not only Jewish and local to the County in which your divorce is pending, but she is also four months pregnant. She would be PERFECT for your case to seek financial damages for the injuries sustained from your husband's assaults on you."*

Although I gave the client this attorney's name and number, the client never placed the call to the lawyer I had recommended. I checked.

She also never contacted me again.

―――――

REPRESENTING FRIENDS presents its own problems.

On one occasion, I represented a friend in his divorce from Wife #3.

Shortly thereafter, I represented his girlfriend, who was entitled to receive an ongoing monthly spousal support award. The fact that she was not receiving any money from her ex was the reason that I became involved in her matter.

One day, I was out with the boys and my friend-client was asked by another friend, *"So when are you getting married?"* They wanted to know when my other client would be his Wife #4.

"Never," I interjected before my client-friend could say a word.

"Why not?"

"Because I won't let her!" I followed with. *"She has too much to lose!"*

Her right to spousal maintenance would have been terminated immediately upon her remarriage. While she was not then receiving all to which she was entitled, the leverage of the claim to both back and future support was too great to give up – at least it was too great for me to give up.

————

THE REPRESENTATION of friends in one thing. The representation of a lawyer is another. The representation of a divorce lawyer is something else entirely.

That has happened twice.

In one instance, the husband and the wife each started their divorce actions against the other. These lawsuits, with one pending in Queens County and the other in Manhattan, were in the infancy of the Equitable Distribution Law, shortly after the effective date of the new statutory provisions.

With there already being trial-level decisions concerning the interpretation of the new Equitable Distribution Law, the rulings between the Courts of these two Counties were inconsistent. Each client had a strategy of selecting the County in which the divorce action was to take place that already had rulings that matched the particular ruling that had already come down.

My client wanted the divorce action in Manhattan, while his wife wanted it in Queens.

Each started an action against the other, selecting the venue that he or she preferred. The two actions started within days of each other.

Ordinarily, the earlier commencement date would control the venue determination.

"Commencement" then would be the date of the filing of the Summons for Divorce; but in order for there to be an action, there needed to be service of that Summons upon the defendant-spouse.

But in this instance, there was an issue of whether personal service of the Summons was ever effectuated.[11]

My client, the husband, claimed that he was never served. The wife's lawyer argued otherwise.

This disputed fact mandated that a "traverse hearing" be held – the name for the limited trials on the issue of service of process.

Ordinarily, these are rather run-of-the-mill hour-long hearings where a process server comes in, testifies that he performed the service, and is cross-examined, after which the defendant testifies that he or she was never served and is cross-examined. In a large majority of these cases, the challenged service is upheld.

What made this case noteworthy is that on this traverse hearing to determine whether my client had been served, there were six witnesses on the hearing lasting two days, five of whom were lawyers, with the sixth being the law student girlfriend of my lawyer client. Even the alleged process server was a lawyer.

What a mess! Not a single witness was believable. So much for the veracity of attorneys.

---

11. Normally, any defect in service could be corrected by re-serving the spouse. However, because another action had been properly commenced, corrective service was not an alternative.

———

THE OTHER CLIENT who practiced divorce law saw the light of day before renewed litigation.

His divorce agreement provided for his alimony obligation to end upon the remarriage of his wife.

His monthly support checks were direct-deposited into her bank account. She moved away to another State; and he had no contact with her whatsoever.

The problem was that neither she nor anyone else (including their adult child) told him when she had remarried. My client continued to pay alimony that he was not technically obligated to pay.

My guy wanted to sue her for the wrongfully accepted over-payments between the date of her remarriage to the date of his discovery of it several months later.

"Are you an idiot?" I said. *"If you go into Court, every other divorce lawyer is going to know that you, a supposedly expert divorce lawyer, were stupid enough to keep paying alimony to a remarried ex-wife. You will be the laughingstock of the Matrimonial Bar."*

"And what happens if you win?" I queried. *"She is unlikely to pay you back and more likely to take an appeal. You have no defense to what became your voluntary continued payments; and even if you did prevail, every lawyer in the State would know how stupid you were because all appellate determinations are public record. And, by the way, what happens if potential clients were to find out? Who would ever retain you after that?"*

Fortunately, my strenuous advice prevailed, with him able to live another day. And it only cost him the few thousand dollars of overpayment. It was a small price to pay to avoid the alternatives.

———

I RECEIVED A CALL one day from an attorney-friend whom I had met years before when she was an adversary counsel. I did not know then that this friend was at that time suspended from the practice of law.

However, the timing of the call should have been a clue to the fact that something was amiss.

"I have this client," she said. *"He is the president of a European subsidiary of a multinational corporation based in New Jersey, with an ex-wife who took him back to Court to increase her alimony."* (This was a New Jersey matter where "alimony" has remained the term of art for spousal support.) The parties had been divorced for a few years before this request for more alimony had been made.

"What's the problem?" I asked, knowing full well that the lawyer (whom I did not know was suspended from practice) would not have referred the matter out unless a problem existed.

"The trial is on Valentine's Day," she told me on February 10th, 1990.

"Wait. You want me to try a support modification case in four days? When will I be able to prepare?"

"Well, he's coming in from Europe tomorrow for the trial, so you have three days to prepare. But he is willing to pay a five-figure retainer fee."

I took on the case and spent most of the next few days learning about the facts of the case and learning about my client. Fortunately, he was both a nice guy and a man who worked his way up the corporate ladder on the financial side, last working as a Chief Financial Officer of this subsidiary before moving on to becoming its Chief Executive Officer. He also was able to explain in clear English the numbers and the tax ramifications of an American earning money outside the country who was subject to income taxes having to be paid both in the country where he earned it and also in the U.S. In short, the very nice CEO salary earned elsewhere, after being taxed twice, was not quite as bountiful as the raw numbers would have suggested. We also had his accountant available to testify as to the specifics of his tax returns, each of which was offered in evidence.

During these few days before trial, I introduced myself via telephone to opposing counsel and quickly learned that a negotiated resolution was a non-starter for his client.

So, we are as prepared as possible given the time constraints when we appeared before the New Jersey Judge handling the matter on Valentine's Day morning. (Although my client was by then an American ex-patriot living exclusively in Europe, the divorce case had been in New Jersey, which had continuing jurisdiction over the support issues.)

The ex-wife, who had the burden of establishing a financial basis for her request for upward modification, went first.

The trial proceeded all day long, first hearing the ex-wife and then with my client on the witness stand. We got to about 4:00 o'clock in the afternoon; and it became painfully apparent that we were nowhere close to concluding the matter by the end of the business day.

My client had reservations to fly back to Europe the following morning.

It seemed to me we would get another trial date a few weeks or months in the future in which to complete the trial.

Instead, the Judge, who had two dozen red roses in a vase on her Bench, told us, *"I already have my roses. The Defendant is flying back to Europe tomorrow; and we are going to finish this today. I don't care how long it takes."*

This, of course, meant to the lawyers, *"Hurry up and get your evidence in; and do it as fast as possible."*

Unbelievably, given the strength of the union representing the Court Officers (and no Judge ever allows any case, let alone a family matter where emotions routinely run high, to proceed without the guy with the gun present in the room), the Judge was able to get her Court Officer to stay in the Court Room until 6:30 p.m.

Both sides rested; and the Judge allowed each side a short time to submit written summations.

The Court them rendered a decision that granted an increase in alimony. The amount of the increase was not nearly as large as my client expected to pay. It was nowhere near what the ex-wife wanted and expected to receive.

The case was over, or so I thought.

But 1990 was not the end of the story.

Every two or three years, the ex-wife, using a different law firm, brought my client back to Court seeking further upward modifications in her alimony. Perhaps because of the status and income of my client, the ex-wife had no problem securing representation by a veritable Who's Who of the Matrimonial Bar in the State of New Jersey.

Each time, my client returned to my office to entertain new motion practice, more evidentiary hearings, and, ultimately, an appeal.

This did not entirely shock me since, during my years with Ira, he had told me about a famous and prolific author of fiction who faced support modification applications every single time a new novel was published or the film rights to an existing novel were sold.

What was unusual about this case was both the length of the representation and the sheer venom of the ex-wife. Although there were three children of the parties' marriage, the marriage itself had been barely ten years in duration. My client had fallen in love with and married his secretary. Even after my client had been married to his second wife for more than 20 years, the ex-wife refused to let go of her woman-scorned emotions.

After this matter proceeded from the initial 1990 post-judgment of divorce modification proceeding, the wife was represented by the crème-de-la-crème of New Jersey matrimonial bar, all of whom knew each other well, spoke, and learned – or at least *should have* learned – about the nature of their client.

Still, she would neither stop litigating against my client nor allow her lawyers to discuss a settlement.

This went on for almost twenty more years! Sometimes, she received a small increase; more often, she was denied any further relief.

At one point, we engaged in settlement negotiations because my client was willing to buy out the entirety of his future payments of lifetime alimony. (While changes to the law were made subsequent to the divorce of the parties, which had taken place in the 1980s – changes that would have called for limited duration alimony for the short-term marriage of these parties – the obligation of my client to pay alimony was permanent subject to termination only on the death of either party or the remarriage of the wife.). My client's second wife became terminally ill; and he had lost all patience with his ex.

At a meeting in her then-newest lawyer's office, the ex-wife voiced the following: *"Women in my family live to the age of 105. I want a payment that would take me to my 110th birthday."*

I immediately asked for a short private meeting with my client. We agreed that further negotiation would be futile; and we walked out of the meeting.

Eventually, we arrived at Labor Day weekend 2009.

By then, many things had changed, both for the parties and for me. Indeed, the Judge who had been assigned to this case had retired, causing reassignment of the matter to another Judge; and then that Judge retired causing yet another reassignment.

The children of these two people had grown up and become emancipated; in fact, each was married with children of his and her own. The medical condition of my client's second wife had deteriorated to such a degree as to cause my client to retire from work and devote himself to the care of his loved one. While he never wanted this litigation to continue – indeed, he never wanted anything to do with his former wife – he wanted this matter over and done with, once and for all.

Things had also then changed for me as I had become separated from my wife at the beginning of 2009; and I was enjoying being a single man in my 50s (which was considerably different from before my marriage when I was a single man in my 20s – which in itself could be the subject of a whole other book).

Depositions (pretrial testimony taken in an office before a Court Reporter where one party is under oath and questioned by the other side's lawyer) were directed by Court Order to take place on the day after Labor Day. Prior deposition dates had been rescheduled on numerous other occasions when, each time, the ex-wife fired her top-tier lawyer only to replace that lawyer with another equally prominent lawyer. The day after Labor Day was set as the proverbial "drop dead" date; the first wife was to depose my client, or she would be deemed to have forever waived her right to do so.

During the week before Labor Day, her then-lawyer became unavailable to me. I could not get him on the phone; nor would he return my calls; nor could I get any information from his secretary.

I did not know if we were proceeding on Tuesday or not.

This left me having to prepare for the questioning of the ex-wife during the three-day Labor Day weekend.

Needless to say, this put a damper on my ability to enjoy my renewed bachelordom – and I had personal plans for most of those 72 hours.

First thing Tuesday morning, I received a call from the secretary to the ex-wife's lawyer telling me that her boss was *"out of the case"* and that I *"should not come to the[ir] offices for the depositions."* Needless to say, I memorialized these statements in an email before I told my client not to show up – I knew better than to risk a future statement that *I had simply not shown up*, making sure that the wife's next lawyer could not Blame Bloom for missing the drop dead date.

A few weeks after that, the case was again before the Court. The attorneys went into the Judge's Chambers to conference the case to advise the Court as to the status of the case. I was still perturbed about the ex-wife having interfered with my Labor Day holiday; and the Judge who knew me well (he was the same Judge who had had a vasectomy performed by my earlier client, the urologist) picked up on my angst over the matter. I had no problem explaining in detail how this woman had impacted my holiday. Surprisingly, neither the Judge nor the newest lawyer for the wife interrupted me.

After further discussion, the Judge made it very clear that this was to be settled *"or else"* (although I was never really sure about what "or else" meant).

Weeks thereafter, my client agreed to make a single payment of one million dollars to his ex (paid through her lawyer) to end his obligations to her.

So ended the twenty-year representation of a client as well as the twenty-year annuity that I had been receiving in fees. I had never before represented a client that long; I never would again.

———

NOT OFTEN DOES A LAWYER have a potential client come into the office when he *knows* the issues are so noteworthy that they cannot help but make law (and make news). Sometimes, cases make law for reasons that no one would expect. But on one occasion, there was no doubt in my mind.

A friend had a coworker who had entered into an arrangement whereby she had been impregnated carry to term the fetus for a gay couple.

Nothing was formal. There was no written contract. She had been impregnated via a turkey baster with the sperm of one of the two fathers-to-be.

She carried the baby to term; and the child was born.

Then she changed her mind. She did not want to give up "her" baby.

As we lawyers are fond of saying, *"Litigation ensued."*

The facts were novel. The law was uncharted, other than for the amorphic standard of "best interests of the child."

Mom hired me. The Dads hired another lawyer.

The case came to Court where I predicted to the Judge that this case would ultimately wind up on the first page of The *New York Law Journal,* the weekday publication addressing all issues of law in the State. I also thought that the case would also be of interest to the mainstream media.

"No, no," said the Judge, *"We will get this settled."*

The case went on. Motion practice occurred as the parties could not agree on anything. A lawyer was appointed for the child. The two Dads were ultimately each required to have independent representation (which probably should have been the case from the beginning, as one had rights as a biological parent that the other did not share).

Mom then fired me and hired the first of several new lawyers. Indeed, each party went through more than one lawyer before the same Judge was forced to render a decision.

Ultimately, the case appeared on the first page of the *Law Journal,* just as I had originally predicted.

CHAPTER 20
TABOOS

I HAVE ALWAYS BEEN A RABBLE-ROUSER. I can never wait to address a controversial topic.

Sometimes that is a good thing. Sometimes, not so much.

As you have read, I have not hesitated to throw myself under the proverbial bus to get the heat off of my client – even to the extent of causing a Judge to have me handcuffed and removed from his Courtroom.

When I was doing my radio show, *The Divorce Hour*, each Friday for over 100 shows, the desire to discuss themes that others wouldn't address proved beneficial and resulted in a go-to interview where I literally scooped the broadcast television networks.

As I mentioned earlier, getting new clients is the most difficult aspect of maintaining a divorce law private practice. One of the ways I tried to get new business was to network. Not an unusual thing. I was part of various networking groups – groups related to divorce, groups related to law in general, groups where like-minded business owners met on the golf course, as well as other types of networking. Through that networking, I met an acupuncturist who was a miracle worker as he was able to literally fix a broken bone in my foot, giving me immediate relief from a pain so severe I could not walk. He and I became friends. In addition to me becoming a patient of his (as well as his most vocal referral source), he, too, used my services and referred me to others. It was a great working relationship.

This acupuncturist had the same zest for identifying and securing new business; and he dabbled creatively in that regard. He developed an internet radio show with topics ranging far and wide, eventually having me on as a guest to address divorce issues. I had a great time as there was nothing I liked more than talking about divorce. Some months later, he expanded into a radio network and offered me the opportunity to speak weekly about anything I wanted to relative to divorce, which, at that time, coincided with my separation and ultimate divorce from my wife of 25 years.

During each of my more than 100 shows, I talked about one topic, usually with a single guest interview, that interested me not as a divorce lawyer, but as a divorce client. I was personally at a crossroads from a devoted family man to returning to a single life; and many topics were of increasing importance to me. I read books; then I interviewed the author. Only the "law shows" when I addressed strictly legal or tax issues (always with a qualified tax expert) were the shows that were drier and thus less than satisfying for me.

Indeed, I thought that doing the show in that manner might well spark curiosity from prospective clients. I repeated my phone number several times during each hour of broadcast; and my shows remained podcasts on the network's website. Those shows remain available on *The Divorce Hour* page of my website, www.divorcebybloom.com.

But I was in error. Notice of my show was largely provided to my own network of clients, professional colleagues, friends, and family, as well as to those that others sent them to. I was just preaching to the choir.

I had hoped for the show to be a client- and fee-generating venture. After more than two years of weekly shows, without a single new client nibble, I realized that no matter how enjoyable the show was, it was not appropriate to continue. While the weekly hour on the air had become the most enjoyable hour of my week, the lack of business did not justify the hours of preparation that the show required. I treated each show as I treated each case; I was fully prepared. After all, I was not going to interview an author without reading his or her book.

There were, however, certain benefits to the show. I had dates with two different listeners. I read things that I would not have otherwise encountered, learning, for instance, about the science and art of kissing from the alternate sources of a biology professor at a major university and Seventeen Magazine. Indeed, I read a lot of non-fiction looking for topics on divorce and life after divorce.

Throughout my life, I have always said that some of the most important lessons that I ever learned were from elementary school. My favorite example of this is the letter-to-the-author assignment in elementary school, where each child was instructed to write a letter to the author of a book that the student particularly enjoyed. The responses were far more frequent than one would have thought.

Well, during the days of *The Divorce Hour*, I did the 21st-century version of that old-school assignment: I sent emails to the publisher. In one instance, I sent an email to the management of a famous singer-songwriter in the hope of an interview to discuss the background for writing what I believe to be one of the most heartrending pieces of music of all time. Although I sent numerous emails to her "people," no response ever came; hence, I will not mention that entertainer here even though, to me, it was the "one that got away."

The other two times I sent a letter to the author/email to the publisher, the results were more positive.

I had happened upon the psychologist author of the custody book, contacted the publisher, and was able to reach the writer. He came to the studio (in a designated area of what had been the acupuncturist's office before he sold his practice – to move to Thailand to become a Buddhist monk!!! Like I said, a very unusual and special guy) for a very interesting hour.

As with every in-person interview, I spent another hour or so before each week's show in my "green room," which in this case was the bagel shop on the other side of West 72nd Street in Manhattan. We talked about him, about the topics I wanted to emphasize as well as those topics he wanted me to hit upon. With time left before crossing the street for the actual interview, we talked about our personal lives. The subject got around to my own separation and divorce, as well as the fact that this experience had altered my perspective on handling divorce cases in general. He reminded me that he had a regular blog on the *Psychology Today* website and offered me the opportunity to write a guest blog, which shortly thereafter became *How My Divorce Made Me a Better Divorce Law*. Googling my name and *Psychology Today* will lead the reader to this article.

What's so taboo about this?

Nothing so far.

But there was another more interesting instance where the email-to-the-publisher ploy paid dividends.

I had been to a family Hanukkah party at the home of one of the three adult sons of my girlfriend. At the time, each of those sons had wives and children (with divorce ultimately hitting one of those households). During the party, the three daughters-in-law were engaged in an animated discussion. Their mother-in-law (my girlfriend) ventured over to see what the girls were talking about; but they seemed embarrassed to discuss the topic with her. Later on, I went over to see what all the fuss was about. Each refused to talk to me about the subject of their banter. *"You know,"* I said, *"Clamming up about his just makes me want to know more about whatever it is you are talking to each other about. The more you refuse, the more I will be intrigued and will not let it go."* After a back and forth, these three women, each hovering on either side of 40, finally admitted that they were talking about a book they had read. After more pulling of teeth, they admitted that the book was *Fifty Shades of Grey*; but they adamantly refused to talk with me or even their mother-in-law about why it had captured their respective attention.

We went home and bought a copy on Amazon. Jo read it first and then gave it to me to read. At that point, the second book of the trilogy had been published; and we each read that as well.

Not really my thing, but all of a sudden, I kept hearing other 40ish women discussing the book. Now that I knew something about its subject matter, I was able to ask questions and engage in a knowledgeable conversation as to the buzz surrounding this book, while still avoiding the obvious potentially embarrassing graphic aspects of it.

I kept coming back to the same question over and over again: Why was there an apparent universal craze among women about this sexual fantasy?

Well, who better to ask than the author herself? I emailed the publisher and got an almost immediate response from the author. We talked on the phone: she was from London, me from New York. I wanted to interview her. *"I never spoke with a man other than my husband about my work,"* she noted in a way that I could tell was hesitant. *"No, no, I don't want to talk about the particulars of the book; and definitely nothing graphic. I want to address the phenomenon of the book, the frenzy it has caused, and about why, it seems, every woman is talking about it."* We then spoke more about this and to convince her that I was not a pervert, explaining the nature of my show, the topics addressed on it, and the fact that seemingly every woman I have come across was enthralled by the book. We also talked about logistics, as I was fully prepared to conduct the interview telephonically. But she was, she said, coming to New York anyway, and would be happy to meet with me in-studio for a personal interview.

Not only was this one of my more enjoyable interviews, but it was unquestionably my greatest "ratings success." She had shared notice of the upcoming interview, her first on our side of "the pond," with her vast network as well as that of her publisher. The new producer of the show, having bought the business from my friend before leaving for Thailand, had equipment where he could track the thousands of live listeners and from where they were located – which, in this case, was literally on every continent other than Antarctica.

I was talking about one of my favorite things: women and sex, and their fantasies. And people were listening!

Later on, I watched others in the traditional media interviewing my "find." I beat CBS; I beat NBC; I beat ABC. I beat CNN and the tabloids. I watched them all; and I could immediately tell which interviewers had not read her books.

It was gratifying; and it was all because:

1. I would not accept "no" for an answer when the girls were giggling between themselves about sexual fantasies; and

2. I never forgot about the letter-to-the-author lesson learned in grade school; and

3. I was not afraid to publicly broadcast about a subject that most would consider taboo.

Another taboo subject that I have never been shy to address is the concept of marriage itself.

"Marriage for life," "until death do us part," was a wonderful concept in its day.

Of course, a committed exclusive lifetime arrangement was most likely developed in the caveman days. But back then, the human life expectancy did not exceed one's thirtieth birthday.

The caveman's "lifetime" relationship was necessarily limited by his expected life.

Times have changed, and we humans live far past our thirtieth birthdays, often doubling and even tripling our life expectancy.

However, societal views regarding marriage have not changed even in the face of a human being's lifetime, which has extended decades longer than before. The marital vow remains unchanged.

Does marriage for life still make sense?

I have argued that if we are to live with monogamy, it should be serial monogamy, where we have different romantic partners, one at a time, who are more compatible with our changing needs over different and evolving changes in our lives.

For this reason, I have suggested at various times and in varying ways, including during my radio show days, that marriage should be a five-year renewable contract.

I am not suggesting that a marriage should end after each five-year term. In fact, I would think that there often should be a renewal of the marriage contract for another five years. Nevertheless, the five-year renewal is an appropriate situation to cause both husband and wife (or husband and husband, or wife and wife) to review the status of their relationship, to see if their respective goals remain aligned, and to evaluate whether another five-year commitment is appropriate for each of the romantic partners.

Much as a marriage does not initially take place unless both parties say *"I do,"* so, too, should there be mutual consent as each new five-year contract is entered into. If one says, *"I don't,"* there would then need to be a discussion of how to end the union as well as how to co-parent the children of this non-tenured union where necessary.

This requires communication between the two partners in the marriage. Conversations and other communication, including communication during sex, are all too lacking as each five-year phase of the marriage comes to an end. The conversations should be a renegotiation of the marriage.

This does not mean an automatic divorce (and all of the legal ramifications thereof), nor does it mean an automatic renewal of the marriage contract. What it means is that there is a commitment on the part of both people to talk about what each wants out of the relationship. This commitment to communication could well result in the strengthening rather than a termination of the relationship.

Think about what I am saying here. Roughly every five years or so, a couple is experiencing new life stressors.

"Honey, our five-year contract is coming to an end. Should we pick up our options? What, if anything, do we need to change if we are going to renew?"

The first five-year stretch is the honeymoon phase when we are young and optimistic. Shared dreams and goals are common in this part of the relationship. Compared to later stages of marriage, when there are children and other divergent career priorities, and when sexual experimentation and physical excitement between the young married couple is replaced with the tried and true.

Five years into the marriage, there is usually a young child whose demands change the focus of each of the parents. On those occasions when the young married couple has time to themselves (and both are awake), the conversations are largely baby-centric.

Often, in this stage of the relationship, one of the married partners becomes the primary parent, and this is true even when both
parents return to work following the birth of the child.

This first five-year phase may set the couple on different
paths, or moving at separate speeds on the same path. The
conclusion of this first five-year period usually presents a road-
block where the couple is faced with how to go around it as one
insists on going left while the other demands to go right, or
where one may want to go over it, under it, or through it. There
may also be instances where one or both of the spouses may view
the obstacle as insurmountable, requiring an end to their journey
together.

The end of the second five-year period coincides with the
couple having more than one child (although I have always
personally believed that an individual should never have more
children than he/she has hands – another matter about which I
fully expect an argument – but with two children the parents can
play one-on-one defense but the minute there is a third or even
fourth child, the parents are compelled to play a zone defense
running the risk that one of the children will be uncovered). How
do we parent together? What is the best way to divide and
conquer? When am I with the younger and you the older? When
am I with the older and you the younger? When do I have both?
When do you? How do we each manage our careers while we
meet the needs of our growing family?

It is another appropriate interval for reviewing where each
party to the marriage is on the road of life.

After five more years, at least one of the children is in school.
In the event that one parent has sublimated his or her career for
the benefit of providing more intensive child care, is it now time
to consider a readjustment of priorities to allow for a refocusing
on his/her career? And if so, how will the other partner adjust
focus to make up for the change of focus of the first?

This ten-year mark requires reevaluation and discussion.

A marriage consists of two people acting as a unit. Where am I? Where are you? Where are we?

Are you going to continue working? Are you ever going to go back to work, and if so, when?

Indeed, each five-year period involves other considerations concerning attention to the children, the specifics of what each spouse envisions for each child, the changing demands of the career of each spouse (particularly when one or both spouses have his/her own business), and ultimately retirement. When one marries, often in their twenties or thirties, they may well consider having children and having careers, but who really considers (or ever consciously thinks about) what will happen at age 65 or what other age they view as appropriate for retirement? Are they to be hands-on grandparents or long-distance grandparents? Will they relocate to another town, State, or country? I submit that no newlywed under the age of 60 consider those options. But say the married couple are 65 years old (or 70, or whatever), and one wants to enjoy his/her golden years in retirement while the other loves working so much that he/she plans to work "forever?" Or the couple both want to continue working (or both want to retire at the same time), but one envisions working remotely from Florida or Portugal while the other has no intention of ever leaving Manhattan? The five-year renewal option forces a serious discussion on how their relationship is to continue, or if it is to continue at all.

This is not an argument where this one particular divorce lawyer (me) simply wants to increase revenue. It is one where we all need to take a good hard look at what marriage is, and what each of us truly wants from a partner. What we want from a partner, I submit, changes over the course of a lifetime, sometimes several times over.

If a person picks the perfect partner, there may well be *pro forma* renewals of their relationship every five years. But even in such cases, the five-year renewal option will provide a distinct opportunity to reevaluate what he wants for himself, what she wants for herself, and what they want as a couple.

———

THANKFULLY, gay marriage is now the law of the land. Love has no boundaries; and recognition of love should never have been categorized where some types are allowed while other types are not. But the law wasn't always that way.

I was always in favor of gay marriage; but I was one of the few who based those feelings on non-political reasons.

Back in the early 1980s, I served on the legislation committee of the family law section of one of the County bar associations. At that time, we were to review pending legislation concerning civil unions, which served as a precursor to gay marriage, ostensibly to provide health insurance coverage and related rights of couples choosing to be in a committed relationship that was not marriage. The enactment of this legislation allowed for the gay couple to be covered on the health insurance policy of one of them, just as a married couple could both be covered under the policy of one and the entire family could be covered under one.

The civil union was not just for gay people. I had a cousin who was in a committed nonmarital heterosexual relationship that took advantage of the civil union option (an option that nevertheless required government filings and formalities) as they did not then wish to marry. [They have since married in the traditional sense.] Their civil union allowed them to both be covered under the health insurance plan of one of them during a time when they were not yet ready to marry.

While on this committee four decades ago, I voiced the following sentiment, *"Why can't we just let them get married?"*

My co-committee members argued against it because of what they perceived as the impossibility of getting political approval.

I supported my argument with the quip, *"Why can't gay people be as miserable as the rest of us?"* But this semi-comedic assertion was merely to mask the non-political reasons underlying my very early support of gay marriage. Those reasons were purely economic.

Simply stated, the more people that were entitled to get married, the more potential divorce clients that would be available in the long run.

Over the next forty years, gay marriage has been recognized as the law in all fifty States.

And during this time, I have had my share of gay divorces.

———

THERE IS ALSO THE TABOO of whether there should be marriage at all.

Couples are getting together, living together, and having children together, with the concept of marriage either being delayed or disregarded in its entirety.

I do not believe that there will be divorce in another 50 years because I truly believe that the concept of marriage itself will become extinct as an unnecessary social structure.

The divorce lawyer will never be a dinosaur, since there will always be children's issues and support issues, as well as issues of property distribution arising at the end of a relationship whether the parties have been married or not.

There will be an evolution of the divorce lawyer's role (one of which may well be the discontinuance of the words "divorce" and "matrimonial"), but as I have attempted to illustrate in this writing, there has always been evolution. We have adjusted to breakthroughs in science which have eventually been recognized in the law. We have adjusted to legislative changes that have required that lawyering include formulaic mathematical calculations. We have adjusted to other legislative changes, which first expanded grounds for divorce and then eliminated the ability to contest the divorce relief itself.

The divorce lawyer will simply evolve. While we will continue to change the nature of our work and probably even undergo a change of name, it seems likely that when the world ends, the divorce lawyer, much like the cockroach, will still roam the globe.

———

THERE IS ALSO THE QUESTION of the wife's resumption of her prior surname (her maiden name or perhaps a married last name from a prior marriage, which might be preferable to her if she had children with that last name).

In New York, at the end of every Judgment of Divorce, there is a clause provision authorizing the wife to use a particular prior surname. Not only is it automatic requiring the wife to do nothing further, but the Clerk will not process a Judgment of Divorce (and thus not finalize the divorce) without this language.

In New Jersey, the spouse has to ask for the resumption of a prior surname. However, so long as the spouse gives sworn testimony (either in Court or in an Affidavit) claiming that she is not seeking the name change for the purpose of avoiding criminal process or for the purpose of avoiding creditors, the name change goes through without a problem. In New Jersey, if the divorce goes through without the name change, and the wife later decides she wants her old name back, she must bring on a formal proceeding to change her name.

The wife is authorized to use the prior name; but she is not required to do so.

But she didn't have *"my"* name before she married me, many men have argued, *"she must take her own name back."* It does not work that way.

My wife and her sister, with a maiden name consisting of a conglomeration of C's and Z's, each married a man with a mono-syllabic last name. Neither was required to *"give the new name back"* upon their respective divorces. Should they have been required to have done so?

———

THE FOLLOWING CASE was not mine. It involved the divorce of my neighbors in the small town where I raised my family. The story was related to me by another lawyer when he heard where I lived and that I knew the parties socially.

The lawyer was representing his long-time friend who was the husband in the divorce.

His client asked as part of the property distribution that one of his wife's breast implants that he had paid for during the marriage be returned to him.

While I am capable of asking for a lot of things on behalf of a client, I do not believe I would have ever had the gumption to ask for that.

———

BEING A BORN RABBLE-ROUSER (and if you don't believe that, try talking to members of my condominium Board of Directors), I was never afraid to cause a little trouble.

The discussion I had with my former wife after she read a client's "story," as previously described, is evidence of that.

But there were other times when I pushed the proverbial envelope in discussions with my wife and with others. That propensity on my part may well have been a cause for my eventual divorce.

My job has always been more lucrative in stories than financial remuneration.

Often, I have been asked the *"Would you represent so-and-so?"* question. This was particularly a topic during the early stages of my career when I was asked, *"Would you represent Joel Steinberg?"* His abuse and eventual murder of his daughter Lisa was particularly heinous and the *cause-celebre* in the late 1980s. On at least one occasion, his case, with the accompanying media frenzy, was in a Manhattan courtroom while I had another matter on the calendar in a different Part on the same floor in the same courthouse. This was much like the criminal attorney being asked, *"Would you represent O.J.?"* (Or, at the risk of alienating the reader, *"Would you represent Trump?"*)

Would I represent Joel Steinberg? In truth, probably not because of the criminal (as opposed to exclusively family law) aspects of his case. But that fact did not deter me in response.

"Everyone is entitled to a legal defense," I would tell my wife even though I knew anything, but an adamant *"of course not"* would have been unacceptable. While I believed and still believe that everyone is entitled to a legal defense, I knew then, as I knew when I said the same thing to friends asking the same question, that I would not want such a case.

But would I leave the needle there? Not when I had the chance to twist it.

"Well, what is the retainer fee? If the fee were large enough, it might be worth taking the case."

––––––––––

THERE IS ALSO A HYPOTHETICAL CASE that, for decades, I described as my "dream case." I have never come across this particular fact pattern in my practice, in the legal treatises, nor in the media. But those facts could very well exist in the course of family practice.

However, whenever I discussed my "dream case," the reaction has been palpable. My wife would stop talking to me. Virtually every woman would be outraged. (I am not sure that most men would not be equally enraged.)

It is, in my opinion, the ultimate taboo.

Roe V. Wade had been the law of the land since 1973 (years before my admission to the Bar in 1980); and it would remain the law of the land until eviscerated most recently by the United States Supreme Court, during the period my practice was concluding and I was in the process of retirement.

Without addressing the politics of abortion (and being a Northeast Jewish Liberal – not to mention my use of the word "eviscerate," I think you can guess my political views on the topic), some of my views have a different slant probably because of my experience as a family law attorney.

The media has identified one side of the debate as being one of "a woman's right to choose." It is a woman who carries a fetus. No, the Courts should not be interfering with how a woman treats her own body.

However, what about Dad? Is it not his body, in connection with hers, that brought about the fetus?

The father of a child has rights and responsibilities, most of which start at birth. This is undeniable whether the father is married to the mother or the couple is unmarried.

Indeed, once a man is adjudicated to be the father, his obligations extend before the birth of the child, as he will be obligated to contribute to the medical and other prenatal costs of the mother-to-be.

"I didn't want the baby," or *"She told me she was on the pill,"* or *"The condom broke,"* or even, *"I withdrew,"* are not valid defenses to a support obligation arising where a child is born after the

sexual act. No one would ever say it was (other than the man trying to avoid his financial obligations arising from the sex act).

The father also has rights

While parental access rights of the father may well be curtailed during the early stages of infancy, particularly during nursing, there is no doubt that the father has a right to see his child even as a newborn. The child has a right to be nurtured by both of his or her parents.

Interestingly, a best-interests-of-the-child analysis is applicable on custodial and visitation issues; although there is no such analysis when the issue is child support. Child support is consistent with the best interests of the child. Every child needs to be supported by both its mother and its father; otherwise, the State must provide for that child.

Self-editing my normally crass assessment, sex makes babies. It is the number one cause of babies (perhaps the *only* cause). Two people created the pregnancy.

(As you can see, I have not addressed the rights of the "fetus," the rights of the child. This is a religious issue and an area well beyond the scope of my so-called "dream case.")

But what about terminating the pregnancy?

I believe that since the decision to have a child – or at least the decision to perform an act that may well result in the creation of a child – is a two-person decision, then the decision to terminate the pregnancy should be a two-person decision as well.

The mother and the father should be the ones involved in the decision to abort, whether for health reasons, for maturity reasons (of the parents, or lack thereof), for financial reasons, for any other reason, or, quite frankly, for no reason.

Politically and from a religious perspective, when the prospective parents agree to terminate or to bring the child to term, that should be the end of it. The State should not be involved; the church should not be involved. The only other involvement should be that of the medical professionals.

But what if the prospective parents disagree?

It is not, I submit, a women's issue alone. It should not be her decision alone since she did not create the fetus alone.

No, I do not think that a father should determine that a woman, wanting to bring her baby to term, should not be compelled by the (alleged) father to terminate that pregnancy.

No, I also do not think the mother's life should be jeopardized when medical complications arise.

And even I could never argue that the rapist would have veto power over the decision to abort his creation.

But then there is my hypothetical dream case. A man comes into my office, married or unmarried. (In my opinion, the marital status of the parties should not factor into the analysis, just as that status has no bearing on the issue of child support.) He tells me that he and his partner (wife or girlfriend) are pregnant and that he is looking forward to becoming a father. He also tells me that, unfortunately, the mother has told him she wants to abort the fetus (in an instance where there are no health concerns for the mother or fetus).

He wants his child and is willing to raise this child by himself if need be.

What are the rights and responsibilities of the parties? (That is a phrase posed repeatedly in Law School.)

This was the case I always wanted to litigate: a case where the woman who suffers from no physical impairment simply does not want this child – or, at the very least, does not want HIS child.

Imagine the legal issues, the equal protection arguments.

Imagine the controversy.

These are the things that this (now retired) litigator could really have sunk his teeth into.

This is also the ultimate in rabble-rousing.
It is the ultimate taboo.

CHAPTER 21
RETIREMENT

Over the course of time, and after my own divorce, I was losing interest in the practice of contested matrimonial litigation,

After more than forty years of legal practice, we were all quarantined due to the COVID-19 pandemic.

During this time, I also learned that my oldest friend and another close friend who each had "beaten" cancer six years earlier, had a recurrence of their cancers.

I very quickly decided that I was not going to work until either I died or was so sick that I could not enjoy a retired life. I never intended to work forever; and life events illustrated my own inevitable mortality.

Because my own divorce lawyer honored the only instruction that I had given him that I be able to retire *someday* following the divorce – and because my life post-divorce was more financially prudent than was my and my wife's marital lifestyle – I did the math and found that with Social Security, as well as retirement and other savings, I was able to enjoy a modest retirement.

With word of the two cancer diagnoses of my friends, I

decided that I would not take on new matters, effective immediately.

However, that left a still fairly filled client list of active matters.

Ultimately, it would take almost another full two years to clear the deck of pending matters as I did not want to abandon any client.

The problem was the pandemic. While in the beginning, there were no physical appearances in Court, within the first year, a single County in my two-state practice resumed personal court appearances in the Courthouse. Everywhere else, conference calls and Zoom-like appearances were the norm; and I was able to appear regularly for conferences, motions, and even some trials without ever having to get dressed below the waist.

The one County that wanted personal appearances was Middlesex County with the Courthouse in New Brunswick, New Jersey. At the time, I still had two pending cases in Middlesex.

However, by that point, I had also moved out of New Jersey and in with the love of my life on Long Island. Appearing in Court in New Brunswick was a logistical nightmare and one that was not on my list of things that I wanted to do.

When a set of motions was scheduled to be heard in one of these Middlesex cases (and with a motion, there is almost always a cross-motion for some relief from the other side) became scheduled for a personal appearance for oral argument, I telephoned my adversary and told her, *"We need to resolve the motions."* She inquired why to which I responded, *"Because I haven't worn shoes in a year and a half."* Thankfully, we resolved our dispute without the necessity of further judicial intervention and thus without the necessity of me putting on shoes, driving to New Brunswick, or physically appearing in Court.

That was it. I was able to settle one of the remaining two Middlesex cases and I explained to the client the impossibility of continuing contested litigation in that County when I now resided in New York. That client was understanding and happily chose to be represented by another New Jersey lawyer whom I had recommended.

During this time, I was contacted by a former client with whom I maintained a particularly good relationship. She wanted me to represent her cousin in a divorce in Middlesex County.

I explained to my former client that I was in the process of retiring and was not taking on new matters. (I did not disclose that a Middlesex County case would never be an exception.)

The client indignantly stated, "*Well, what are we supposed to do? We need you.*"

I again explained my pending retirement as well as the fact that I had moved to Long Island making appearances in New Brunswick a practical impossibility.

I also offered to refer her and her cousin to the attorney who represented me in my divorce.

"*Is he any good?*"

"*No. He sucks. Of course, he is good. Let me google him so I can give you his number.*"

So, I opened up Google to look up the law firm that represented me during my divorce. (Before I was represented in my case, I was still undecided about whether I would retain my own lawyer or represent myself. The largest matrimonial law firm in the State of New Jersey was a firm with which I was particularly acquainted as I had had matters with four different partners one of whom had an approach to divorce cases that coincided with my own. I did not want this firm to represent my wife. I pulled a Tony Soprano and formally consulted with this lawyer for the sole purpose of having the ability to conflict the firm out in the event that my wife sought to retain them.)

My wife first retained a lawyer that I knew and with whom I maintained a good relationship. As "my" lawyer did not know this particular lawyer, I elected to use my lawyer as a ghost lawyer while technically representing myself to allow me to have direct communications with my wife's attorney. For a few months, this worked well as no formal litigation had been commenced, but also there was no movement towards a resolution of our divorce. One day my wife replaced the lawyer that I knew and liked with another lawyer that I knew but with whom I had a less-than-friendly relationship. I immediately called my lawyer and told him that I was FedEx-ing him a check and advised him that I wanted to start litigation without a moment to lose.

Lo and behold, while doing the googling, I discovered that the lawyer who had represented me was no longer with the firm. I found this hard to believe but reckoned that lawyers change firms all the time. Or maybe he elected to have his own firm.

So, I googled him as opposed to just the firm. *"Oh my God,"* I said in real-time as the computer screen opened, *"Here's his obituary."*

Stunned, I then told the person looking for a lawyer, *"Let me try my wife's second lawyer. She hates me, but she did a really good job for her client."*

I googled this woman only to find, unbelievably, that there was an obituary for her as well.

"Well," I said spontaneously, *"if I wasn't going to retire before, I certainly would be retiring now."* I went on to say, without thinking, *"I know my divorce was rough, but I never thought it was THAT rough."*

I recovered and then referred this potential client to another woman in another firm who was not only particularly knowledgeable but was also a decent human being. It is the same person to whom I later referred my unsettled Middlesex County case as well as all my other inquiries for divorces in the State of New Jersey.

CHAPTER 22
BLAME BLOOM

THERE IS AN OLD ADAGE: *If you don't have the facts, argue the law. If you don't have the facts or the law, argue the lawyer.*

Every lawyer uses this quip. So did I.

Indeed, when I was cuffed at the direction of the Judge, I had been arguing the "Judge."

The goal is to get the attention off of the client. In the "cuffed" case, I knew full well that by making this argument I was taking the attention of the Court away from my client and putting it squarely onto myself.

Over the years, I repeated the adage over and over again, to the point where I got bored with it. It is tough to be effective as an advocate when your heart is not in your remarks.

I realized that I had the perfect alliterative alternative; and it was so simple.

It could be said with feeling, with such sarcasm.

"That's right, Your Honor, just Blame Bloom!"

And then I would go on, *"Let's just forget the facts. Let's forget about what he (or she) did. Let's forget about what he (or she) didn't do.*

Let's even forget about the law. Let's take the easy way out and just Blame Bloom!"

I then listed the particular misconduct of the other side and the failures of the other side to do things that were required of him (or her).

"But let's forget about each of these things because it's just so much easier to just Blame Bloom!"

———

THIS WAS AN EFFECTIVE MEANS of parrying an onslaught of personal attacks over the years.

But then came one of my final cases.

The wife was the girlfriend of one of my former clients whom I had represented a decade or so before.

In January of 2020, she came in with her boyfriend, who had touted my abilities as a lawyer, to interview me about her case. I had represented him without a single problem. Indeed, I was his lawyer from start to finish, just as his wife's lawyer was her only lawyer.

The new client felt that since she had a boyfriend and her husband had a girlfriend, the parties had each moved on, and the divorce would be *pro forma*. She also told me that the parties were *"pretty much"* in agreement.

Even though I had a bad feeling about this being "an easy divorce," and was wary about them being only "pretty much" in agreement, I kept that to myself.

I explained that there was still an agreement that needed to be prepared, that language needed to be carefully drafted both with regard to each party's waiver of spousal maintenance and with regard to a deviation from the child support standards amount of child, and that a mutual waiver of pension rights needed to be specifically drafted. She was earning almost as much as her husband; and she was willing to cut her husband a break on child support since he was agreeing to allow her to relocate with the child from Brooklyn to New Jersey with her boyfriend, who was purchasing a new home for them, a relative short distance but one that involved the crossing of State lines and the continuing need to cross two toll bridges each time the father was to visit his daughter.

I quoted her a fee commensurate with the work to be done factoring in a small discount to my regular hourly rate as a result of the referral from a former client.

Not surprisingly, she decided not to retain me, telling me that she did not need a lawyer to finalize what she believed had already been agreed upon.

Instead, she relied on her husband's lawyer to draft an agreement.

There are many ways a lawyer can represent a party in a matrimonial action. A lawyer is usually retained by a party and paid for by that party. On occasion, particularly in some instances where contempt of court is an issue, and there is a possibility that a litigant would face incarceration, the Court will appoint a lawyer, with that lawyer compensated by the State of New York pursuant to Article 18-B of the County Law. Appointed lawyers are paid at a far lesser hourly rate than retained counsel.

There are also instances when a lawyer is retained with little or no initial fee paid, with the lawyer making an application for an award of legal fees to be paid by the other spouse. Such was how I got the biggest case I ever had previously discussed.

There are times when a lawyer takes on a case *pro bono*, which means that the lawyer is working entirely for free without any expectation of being paid. In both New York and New Jersey, upon regular annual or bi-annual attorney registration, a lawyer is required to disclose the amount of *pro bono* representation he (or she) has provided during the preceding period.[12]

And then there is the union lawyer or the lawyer who is provided to a client as an emolument of his (or her) employment. In other words, the legal fee is not paid by the client, or at least not paid until a threshold of hours of legal work has been performed, but rather is paid by the labor union or the employer.

While the union lawyer has obvious benefits to the party receiving free representation, it is often a disaster for everyone else concerned. Indeed, even though the union lawyer is guaranteed payment much like the Court-appointed lawyer – unpaid legal fees are prevalent among the Matrimonial Bar – the compensation rate is far less than what a privately retained lawyer will be paid when the client is directly billed. While many lawyers have accepted this type of retention, it is usually reserved for the young, struggling, just-starting their own private practice. I should also mention that when Ira and I went our separate ways in the early 1980s, I worked under such an arrangement with one of the large unions in New York City – for a very short time, given the paltry hourly rate and the limited maximum fee or "cap" for each case.

The biggest problem with this type of representation is that the client who is not paying his (or her) own lawyer has no incentive to settle the case. The client who is not directly paying for legal representation can sit back and make demands, and can just say, "no," to any attempt at a negotiated settlement. When there is no cap (or a very high cap) on the number of hours a lawyer under a prepaid legal plan is to be paid, there may also be an incentive on the part of the lawyer to keep the case going.

My personal belief is that representation by the union or

---

12. I recall taking on a pro bono case for a friend of my daughter while they were in high school. The friend was being beaten by his father; and I could not and would not take a fee to protect this teenager. Indeed, I refused a fee even when the Judge reminded me that under the law a fee could have been awarded to me.

company lawyer should be banned. However, that is never going to happen particularly when the representation under these circumstances is the right of the employee and a product of collective bargaining.

However, since it is clearly to the advantage of the so-represented spouse and to the disadvantage of his (or her) spouse, I always argue for the party receiving free representation to have imputed to his (or her) income an amount commensurate with the value of the legal fee that that spouse is not paying directly, that it is additional income to the so-represented spouse. I also always argue in these situations that because one spouse is receiving free legal services, that spouse should be contributing to the legal fee obligation of the other spouse who does not have the same employment benefit.

Reasonable arguments? One would think. But it is almost never accepted by the Court.

So, the prospective client in January 2020 (and the date is important) came in for a price quote for me to represent her to write the agreement and finalize the divorce. That price was not to her liking; she told me she would let her husband's union lawyer take care of the agreement as well as, presumably, the divorce.

Even though she was not retaining me, I had advised her to have some lawyer review the agreement on her behalf. Not surprisingly, she did not.

Instead, she received from opposing counsel in early March of 2020 the proposed Separation Agreement which provided the resolution of all issues between the parties including a mutual waiver of spousal support, child support at a lower than statutory guidelines amount, and custody and visitation, as well as the right for the wife to relocate with the child to New Jersey at the end of the school year.

Much to my later chagrin, my client had agreed to give her

husband "February's off," with the obligation to pay child support eliminated in February of each month. This was something that I would have advised the client against. As I would later argue when seeking a de novo consideration of child support, *"Does the child not eat during February? Does she not need a roof over her head or utilities in February?"*

She and her husband each signed the Separation Agreement in the middle of March with the wife delegated with the task of getting the signed agreement back to her husband's lawyer.

Rather than keeping a photocopy of the signed agreement – as any lawyer for her would have done or at least would have told her to do – she elected to do what she believed was the next best alternative: she used the camera feature of her cellphone and took pictures of each party signing the agreement and of the pages with the parties' signatures and those of the notary's signatures. She already had an unsigned version of the agreement on her computer, having originally received it by email. The wife then went to the post office and mailed the only existing hard copy of the signed Separation Agreement to the attorney for the husband, sending it by regular mail as opposed to certified or registered mail, or anything requiring a return receipt. She used her cellphone camera again to take a picture of the postal receipt.

The date of March 2020 is important because that was the onset of the COVID-19 pandemic. The husband then lost his job, but for reasons never fully explained, he retained his legal services plan.

The lawyer representing the husband had been working for a law firm was furloughed and moved out of State to Texas. Later, that lawyer would come off furlough but remained out of the New York/New Jersey area for most if not all of the relevant time.

Nothing happened with the matter, which was not unexpected because of the closures associated with the pandemic.

The only things that did occur were conversations, emails, and texts between husband and wife about the wife's move with the child from New York to New Jersey. As a result of the lockdown, the child's school was closed later becoming virtual over the computer. Because of this, the wife wanted to advance the scheduled end-of-the-school-year relocation from June to the end of April. The husband agreed, with texts and emails confirming the consent to the relocation; those texts and emails served as evidence of the parties' agreement when the husband later changed his mind.

The move to New Jersey occurred at the end of April.

The husband also stopped paying any child support whatsoever at that time.

Fast forward to late May; and the client returned to my orbit. She called me, not knowing the status of her case or the status of her life. She told me about how she signed the agreement as well as the manner in which she transmitted it to the attorney representing her husband, providing me with the photographs.

I was formally retained. I agreed to accept the originally quoted retainer fee, but that fee would be exhausted trying to undo the damages caused since I first quoted a fee.

My first order of business was to communicate in writing with the attorney to whom my client had mailed the signed Separation Agreement, demanding that I immediately be provided with a copy of it. I also demanded that child support be reinstated immediately and that all past due child support arrearages be satisfied at once.

No response.

At the same time, I was also able to determine the absence in the agreement concerning making certain required statutory representations about the amount of child support that would have been called for based on the respective incomes of the parties had there been a calculation under the child support guidelines – which under the statute also required a representation that the guidelines support amount was "the presumptively correct" amount of child support to be awarded – and the reason or reasons for deviation from the guidelines amount. The absence of this requisite language would have unnecessarily delayed the processing of the divorce because the matrimonial clerk responsible for reviewing the papers would backburner the incorrectly filed paperwork.

Later efforts by me to redraft the agreement to correct these deficiencies took up valuable time as well as costing the client thousands of dollars of what would have otherwise been needless legal fees.

When it became apparent that I was being stonewalled by the other side, I prepared a Summons for Divorce for filing to commence the litigation, as well as a formal motion brought by Order to Show Cause.

The proposed Order to Show Cause was supported by the sworn Affidavit of the client as well as her separate sworn Affidavit of Net Worth, my own Affirmation in which I affirmed under penalty of perjury the truthfulness of my remarks about the relevant law and its application to the particular facts of the case, and various exhibits that provide evidence of the representation made in the Affidavit and Affirmation.

An Order to Show Cause, once signed by a judge, requires the opposing side to come into Court (then virtually by computer link on a Zoom-like hookup), either themselves and/or with counsel, to "show cause" as to why the Court should not enter a formal order requiring that other party to do something. An Order to Show Cause may also include the granting of immediate temporary relief (called a Temporary Restraining Order) under exigent circumstances that warrant an immediate direction by the Court without the other side first having an opportunity to be heard.

In this instance, our Order to Show Cause did not seek any temporary *ex parte* (one-sided) relief. Instead, we sought speed as the Order to Show Cause would get us before the Court much faster than a simple Notice of Motion.

We sought in various combinations or individually the following relief (among other things such as legal fees):

1. The production of the original signed and notarized Separation Agreement; and

2. The immediate resumption of payment of child support under the terms of the Separation Agreement; and

3. The payment of all past due child support that had accrued under the Separation Agreement; and/or in the alternative

4. A new determination by the Court of Child Support, ordering the husband to pay child support in the amount determined to be correct under the application of the child support guidelines (in other words, determining child support *de novo* as if there were no agreement of the parties).

I was aware of the law relative to the necessity of written agreements and what was required for them to be enforceable by a Court. This was the reason that the very first request was for the production of the document that only opposing counsel had in his possession.

Although I acknowledged that I did not have it, the Court was specifically advised that the written agreement did indeed exist. The Court was also advised as to the manner of execution as well as the contents of every page of it, both before and after its formal execution by the parties. I provided photographs and documents. There were, we submitted, no questions about the contents or the obligations detailed in the parties' agreement. It was not a case of, *"He said; she said; it was one of "Here it is!"*

These obligations included the obligation to pay child support (albeit with "February's off). We therefore asked for enforcement of those obligations.

We did not represent that we had either a full copy of the agreement in the traditional sense or any original of it, although we submitted that the terms of the parties' actual agreement were clear and without any question. We also noted that the husband's attorney had the original in his office.

But because of what we did not have, we included the request for alternative relief in the form of a new determination by the Court of what the child support obligation should be.

As would later become part of my submissions to the Court, I argued that not to seek this alternative form of relief under these circumstances would constitute legal malpractice on my part.

In response to the detailed Order to Show Cause, "it" hit the fan.

I received from opposing counsel hundreds of pages of submissions on behalf of the husband including several hundreds of case citations that were claimed to be germane to the issues. Those issues, they claimed, were that there is no agreement; that they don't have the agreement (even though there is a presumption under the law that what was mailed was deemed to be received with the burden of proof shifting to the recipient to establish the mailed document had not been received); that there was no agreement in existence; and, most importantly, that this is all *"Bloom's fault,"* thus necessitating that not only should our motion be denied but that my client and I be formally sanctioned and penalized under the Court Rules and that I, not my client, be required to pay the husband's legal fees notwithstanding that counsel for the husband was being separately paid by a third party under the husband's employment records. In other words, the lawyers wanted to be paid twice, with one of those payments coming out of my pockets as opposed to my client's.

Amongst other things, I advised the Court that there is no provision in statutory or case law requiring a lawyer to pay the legal fees of the opposition client.

This went on for the next eighteen months with a Zoom-like appearance held every couple of months, with the Court carrying the motions without determination.

The husband later threatened to, and then did actually, make a motion requiring that the child be returned to the State of New York even though he had consented to the relocation and the child, who suffered from learning disabilities, had acclimated to the change of residence over more than a year after she moved and was thriving in her new environment.

The case would go back and forth, sometimes reaching a point where an agreement on almost all issues, before the husband went back to demanding the return of the child to New York. I note that there were occasions when *"almost all issues"* were resolved, which required me to rewrite the agreement in its entirety, only to have new objections made when I included recitation of income and calculations of the presumptively correct amount of child support that necessarily needed to be set forth to have a viable agreement.

Furthermore, *"almost all issues"* resolved never reached the point where the husband and his counsel were willing to forego their claims that I personally be required to compensate the defendant's attorney.

Indeed, during a conference with the Court, while I was still involved in the case, everyone acknowledged that all matters were resolved *"except for the claims against Bloom."* When the Judge's Law Clerk heard this, she indicated to the parties and counsel that the Judge was unlikely under those circumstances to award relief against me personally and that without an agreement on everything, there was no agreement.

Still, the husband's attorney refused to withdraw the relief he sought against me.

This was Blame Bloom on steroids.

Finally, it got to the point where I had no choice but to advise my client that *"This case will never settle as long as I remain your lawyer. They hate me too much. Why? I don't know. While I am happy to continue as your attorney, I think you might be better off retaining new counsel."*

Ultimately, she did so. But that is neither the end of the story nor the end of my involvement in this case.

The matter continued with another attorney representing the wife. The husband continued with his same free (to him) lawyer. However, because relief was still being sought against me personally, I requested and was granted permission to appear on my own behalf at further Court appearances.

There were another couple of further appearances on the case, with these each held weeks apart. During these appearances, the same took place as before: the parties agreed to everything except that Bloom should pay the husband's legal fees even though there was no precedent to the granting of such relief. The husband's lawyer made the same remarks while I asserted the same defenses, including the fact that it would have been malpractice for me not to have acted as I did, all the while reminding the Court that I had been replaced and that I was arguing now only on my own behalf and not on behalf of the wife, and that my continued work was without compensation to me. The wife's new lawyer sat silently.

The case kept getting adjourned without resolution until one day when I called the Court to confirm the date and time of another appearance as well as the web address for the virtual Zoom-like conference.

I was told by the Clerk, *"Mr. Bloom, that case has been settled and the appearance has been canceled."*

"No kidding," I replied. *"No one had the courtesy of advising me."*

"By the way," I added, *"what happened to the relief sought against me?"*

"It's been withdrawn."

The case seemed to have taken on a life of its own. The parties thought they had finished their case by this settlement.

However, as "a" lawyer (as opposed to "the" lawyer) on the case, my email address was in the court system, and I had notice of all subsequent developments. Even though the issues were resolved, and even though my former client had become pregnant (with my original former client's child), necessitating motion practice before the Court to advance the divorce matter to the top of the list, and even though the husband consented to the request to expedite the matter, it still took another year and a half to process the final divorce to allow my former client to marry the father of her child. The child was born before that all could happen.

Because of the pandemic? Partially. Because of the volume of divorces in that County? Again, in part. But in my humble opinion – based upon the filings that I still had access to – because of bad lawyering by both my successor counsel and, to a lesser extent, by my adversary.

But who was I to say anything? And who am I to say anything now? No one.

Just Blame Bloom!

AFTERWARD

The worst divorce I have experienced has been not as an attorney but as a family member.

Hands down, my brother's divorce was the worst divorce ever. He did not listen to me. I told him to keep his wife and keep his girlfriend, as his circumstances were very peculiar. For whatever reason, he could not do that. Without getting graphic, in the early stages of his divorce, his wife's boyfriend abused his children, each then under 10, and my understanding is that this individual went to jail because of it. My brother, admittedly no saint, never got past the guilt associated with these life-altering assaults upon his own children and ultimately took his own life. My brother's death, which I still consider to be "on my watch" and for which I myself underwent more than a decade of psychotherapy, has molded my professional career in addition to my personal life.

Some fifteen years after Richard's death, I had to tell my father that I, too, was ending my marriage. My father, albeit older and with the onset of dementia, was still able to connect the dots.

"Dad, my kids are older and what happened to my brother's kids could not happen to mine. But if it did, I assure you that I would be homicidal rather than suicidal."

This, he understood.

———

THE HARDEST DECISION I have ever made in my life was to end my own marriage. I imagine that an even harder decision would be to end an engagement before the wedding. But sometimes, that may be the best of all possible worlds. In retrospect, the only downfall in that is the fact that the children you love so much would never have existed but for the marriage regardless of its ultimate demise.

———

DIVORCE SUCKS. There is no other way to describe it.

I lost one of my clients (and I did not represent my brother) to suicide.

On another occasion, the death under questionable circumstances – was it an accidental overdose, or was it a suicide? – or the wife of a friend whom I was then representing were events that both compounded my distress over my brother and reminded me of the seriousness of the divorce process.

The death of a client's spouse during matrimonial litigation may be, from a professional aspect, *"the best of all possible worlds,"* as there is no longer a question of support or property distribution. But survivors suffer lingering, sometimes life-long psychological ramifications.

Divorce is a serious business.

But divorce is also the most difficult decision one may make.

Indeed, I myself struggled with it for a decade and a half before pulling the trigger and proverbially running away from home.

While my divorce was not a seven-figure fee or even a six-figure one, it was still far more expensive than I had planned and far more expensive than it needed to be.

It was, at least for me, worth every penny of it.

ACKNOWLEDGMENTS

Books do not write themselves; and they are not written in a vacuum.

I have so many people to thank.

The people who have read early versions of this book – in no particular order, Stephanie Pecorino, Marcia Golden, Jo Dichter, Katie Bloom, Jonathan Lissmann, and Jake Bloom – are people I loved before they ever read a page. I would have thought no less of them had they declined my invitation to read and make recommendations. The fact that each was happy to participate in this endeavor is overwhelming.

My good friend David Dukes took the photograph of me that is part of the cover of this book (as well as every other dating profile of me ever used). I can't thank him enough.

A special thanks to my oldest friend, Paul Millman, whose support, encouragement, and advice were not only extraordinary but inspirational. He has convinced me that this memoir could be so much more than a vanity project. Although I joked about his "homework assignments" for me (including the reading of the Louis Nizer book), each task was thought-provoking and made this narrative more readable.

To the late Ira Richard Bennett, I owe my love for the law and my tireless pursuit of it.

The countless referring lawyers and adversaries (and sometimes both) throughout my years as a lawyer have helped me become the advocate and adviser that make up a good lawyer.

Finally, but by no means least, the clients who have literally entrusted me with their lives must be told of my eternal gratitude for their faith in me.

ABOUT THE AUTHOR

Lawrence H. Bloom has been an attorney in New York since 1980 and an attorney in New Jersey since 1984.

He has an undergraduate degree from Cornell University and a doctor of jurisprudence from Albany Law School where he served on and published in the Law Review.

His law practice has focused on divorce and family law.

He resides in Boynton Beach, Florida.

This is his first book.

www.ingramcontent.com/pod-product-compliance
Lightning Source LLC
Chambersburg PA
CBHW051513150726
47997CB00001B/224